Whittlin' and Fiddlin' My Own Way

Violet Hensley

The Violet Hensley Story

Whittlin' and Fiddlin' My Own Way

By Violet Hensley

with Randall Franks

Silver Dollar City's
Whittlin' Fiddler from Yellville

From a Backwoods Farm to National Fame

Whittlin' and Fiddlin' My Own Way
© 2014 Violet Hensley and Randall Franks
Peach Picked Publishing P.O. Box 42, Tunnel Hill, Georgia 30755
http://randallfranks.com/
ISBN: 978-0-9849108-2-3
Editor: Rachel Brown Kirkland

All photo and art copyrights remain with their owners.
Special thanks go to:
Silver Dollar City for numerous promotional photos featuring Violet, including the front cover photo and the use of the Silver Dollar City logo.
www.silverdollarcity.com
Artist Julie Rice, painting of Violet Hensley featured on the back cover.
JulieRice.net
Artist Jack Dawson for his painting of Violet Hensley's homeplace.
http://www.jackdawson.com/
TV personality promotional photos: Russ Scott, Danny Williams, Jack Miller, and Cliff St. James
Other Photos: Violet Hensley Collection, unless otherwise noted
We thank the many family and friends whose talents contributed to the photos included in Violet's collection from throughout her life. We noted photographers whose names were available.

Visit
www.VioletHensley.com

Dedication

I dedicate this book first and foremost to my dad, George Washington Brumley, because he made his first fiddle at age 14 without any patterns or help. Knowing this inspired me to make my first fiddle on my own at age 15, which led to my being called the "Whittlin' Fiddler." Also, I wish to dedicate it to the Herschend Family of Silver Dollar City, Missouri, who provided the venue that exposed me, and my craft, to the eyes of the public. Finally, to my friends Brad and Linda Leftwich, who sent many musicians my way, including Matt Brown who nominated me to be awarded the Mike Seeger Scholarship in 2009 at the Folk Alliance International Conference in Memphis, Tennessee.

Contents

Introduction

When looking at the musical life of Violet Hensley, one must wonder about her career significance in the history of American music. Bluegrass fiddler and vocalist Alison Krauss achieved more Grammys ® than any other female artist in history, but when the Whittlin' Fiddler made her television debut in 1968, such accolades were not the norm. Dolly Parton, Loretta Lynn, Lynn Anderson, Tammy Wynette, and Jeannie C. Riley were among the other female artists seen on TV that year. Most of the stars were 30 years Violet's junior and were the age of her children.

The American folk music revival of the 1950s and 1960s fostered an environment where a 50-year-old backwoods Ozark woman who raised nine kids and crafted and played fiddles could find an avenue to rise from obscurity to the international pop culture stage. When Violet Hensley picked up her father's fiddle and started to play in the 1920s there had only been three female hillbilly performers that had found their way to recordings — Samantha Bumgarner and Eva Davis of North Carolina recording for Columbia, and Roba Stanley of Georgia for Okeh, all in 1924. Fiddler Anita Sorrells at the age of 15 had already broken new ground for women by becoming the first to compete in the Old Time Fiddler's Convention in Atlanta, Ga. where she won second place. She would return in 1931 to take the top prize.

In their little Arkansas community of Alamo, Violet knew of none of these women or their strides for women in the music industry. She did not even have a notion that one day she might share the music she was playing with others as an artist. Neighbors at area gatherings and square dances would be her only audience in the 1920s and 1930s.

The first women she heard playing music on radio or records were Maybelle and Sara Carter performing with A.P. as the Carter Family. Their 1927 Victor recording "Wildwood Flower" impacted her early life. Fiddler and western singer Patsy Montana would be the next woman to influence the young fiddler with her recorded music.

Violet was passionate about making fiddles like her father. The craft fascinated her even more than playing music, and she grew proficient at it.

In a similar experience to contemporary Roba Stanley, Violet gave up excursions as a fiddler in the 1930s after she married; in Violet's situation, it was to appease her husband's jealousy.

Her love of music and fiddle making resurfaced in the late 1950s almost in perfect timing with the era that created a surge of new folk stars such as the Kingston Trio. Women such as Kitty Wells, Jean Shepard, Goldie Hill, June Carter, and Martha Carson were making strides for women in country music.

As Violet stepped back on stage in 1961 in Yellville, Ark., she still did not see herself as a performer, but within six years she became one of the most visible fiddlers in America, and probably the most visible woman fiddler in history up until that time. Fiddler Ramona Jones, who would appear on Hee Haw, was still three years away from the debut of that long-running hit show. Violet reached her audience by sharing her talents on almost every major news, talk, entertainment, variety, and children's show in each market throughout the central United States annually for decades, adding to that performances on numerous major network TV and radio shows. She performed for millions of TV viewers and often gave countless interviews in magazines and newspapers. She encouraged the last of the young baby boomers and the first of Generation Xers to learn more about mountain music. All this was done while encouraging two-plus generations of Americans to travel to Silver Dollar City.

Her ability to charm a TV audience with a twinkle in her eye and a sharp-witted quip on her tongue made her a favorite with TV hosts that kept her coming back year after year. Her stage outside of the TV and radio medium was limited primarily to her public appearances at folk music events, craft fairs, schools, and Silver Dollar City.

In music history, her recordings probably had minimal impact; but as a female fiddler and fiddle maker who came into her own during the rise of the women's movement in America, Violet helped paint a different face on a style of music and a craft many considered a man's domain.

Who knows how many of today's generation of singers and musicians were sitting in front of her appearances on Captain Kangaroo, Bozo the Clown, or many other children's shows?

Randall Franks and Violet Hensley share a tune at Silver Dollar City in 2011.

© 2011 Randall Franks Media – Jerry Robinson, Sr.

Preface

by Randall Franks

The sound of an up tempo version of "Ragtime Annie" emanating from a sweet mellow fiddle pulled my ear from the hallway into the auditorium where I leaned against the wall looking up at a woman in a bonnet play at the International Bluegrass Music Museum's Pioneer Gathering in 2010.

Despite the years she carried, the presence of the instrument seemed to bring out an exuberance that is generally seen only in early youth. I have spent my life seeing the greats of traditional music share their talents as I tried to emulate the best of them in what I do. For some reason though, the spirit that emanated across the room from this small-framed woman in 1880s dress demanded my attention. As applause rang out, she was led off stage and right by me as she held the hand of a young guitarist.

I met her officially at a luncheon for the legends being honored and took a photo of her with Curly Seckler and Ramblin' "Doc" Tommy Scott. Photographer and author Stephanie Ledgin asked me at the International Bluegrass Music Association World of Bluegrass later that year whether I knew Violet and if I might consider picking up on a project that her schedule would not allow — coaxing Violet to bring her life into words for a book. I began thinking about it and pursued the process of calling Violet to open a dialogue. Those thoughts were curtailed when my hometown of Ringgold, Georgia was hit by a devastating tornado that struck 600 homes and 100 businesses on April 27, 2011. As a member of the local emergency planning commitee, my focus shifted for several months to responding to the needs of our community in between movie roles and musical appearances.

Violet and I came to a meeting of the minds, and the process initiated with a visit to Silver Dollar City in Branson in October 2011. My brother Jerry Robinson, Sr. and I drove from Georgia and spent the day with her there, watching her share the talents as she had since the 1960s. Of course, I could not resist playing a few tunes with her as we both entertained the visitors to Silver Dollar City sharing "Little Liza Jane," "Ragtime Annie," and "Liberty." We began a weekly hour-long interview. We reviewed her memories and memorabilia, narrowing it into the story that Violet wanted to tell about her life. Creating the book long distance also meant we had to enlist the assistance of her family members, especially as we came to the point of review and corrections, since Violet's sight is very limited. Thanks to Sandra, Russell, Lewonna, and other diligent members of the family, the work came together.

I want to thank Violet for the opportunity to delve into her walk down the dirt roads of Arkansas and Oklahoma that brought her to stand in front of millions of people from around the world on television, in concert, and at Silver Dollar City. My life has been enriched by listening to her stories of growing up in rural Arkansas. I know yours will be as well when you have read this book.

by Violet Hensley

I never imagined I would be writing a book about my life. My daughters Sandy and Wonnie wanted me to write one. I couldn't bring myself to think on how I would put it to paper.

After a gentleman named Randall Franks contacted my daughter Sandy, and then me, I finally became more serious about writing it, and we got started.

I had to start gathering up where I'd been, who I taught, start finding the pieces of 97 years of life to put in the book. Initially, I found some photos, magazine articles, and then moved on to my journals that I kept at the height of my travels. My journals were more one-line notes than a diary, but they provided a good skeleton of things that struck me at the time.

Throughout the process, I have called on all of my children to refresh my memory on different parts of our story. Beatrice, Marvin, Calvin, Russell, R.G., Eddie, Sandra, Lewonna, and Wilma have all played a role in the process of me pulling the pieces together.

Until I started working weekly with Randall, I never imagined taking the simple things we did from day-to-day and trying to make those interesting for other people, but I hope that I have managed to turn our lives into somethin' that folks will enjoy reading and hopefully learn somethin' from our experiences.

Foreword

Throughout America's history there have been numerous amusement attractions that have become part of the fabric of the patchwork of the American experience.

When Hugo and Mary Herschend leased Marvel Cave near Branson, Mo. in 1950, so began a chapter in history that would change many lives and help raise the spirits of generations.

The Herschends made a choice to build upon the traditions of the region reflected in the 1880s by adding Silver Dollar City and showing craft making to entertain those waiting to visit the cave in 1960. Their decision changed the lives of many traditional craftsmen and craftswomen from throughout the region and established the theme the park would grow upon.

When the park was still in its infancy, among the cast of characters who came to call Silver Dollar City home was a lady who never was playing a part. Instead she simply was herself, reflecting the rural life she lived while captivating millions with her talents — Violet Hensley.

As the attraction grew and became a major amusement park, it introduced millions to the Ozarks and the way of life seen in the settlements of Missouri and Arkansas. The whittling fiddler of Yellville, Arkansas, helped to attract folks to come and see the park by appearing in front of millions on television and radio to herald its attributes.

Peter Herschend, Herschend Family Entertainment co-founder and owner, said Violet is one of their City's most unique citizens.

"In the early years of growing Silver Dollar City, Violet Hensley, Don Richardson, and I, along with an interesting assortment of the City's colorful characters, would spend weeks on the road together...all devoted to promoting SDC," he said. "I came to see Violet Hensley for the amazingly wonderful woman that she is. She would amaze us with stories of field plowing with her mules. Then a new Violet would seem to appear when she would sit for an interview with some grizzled reporter (reporters who probably did not believe she was real), and she would proceed to win them over with her charm, her skills as an artist, her talent as a musician.

"Violet is the wonderful lady that we have had the privilege of knowing.... watching her work her magic with the carving knife.... creating music from what used to be a block of wood.... But most of all, our privilege of knowing a wonderful and unforgettable lady," he said.

His brother Jack Herschend, Herschend Family Entertainment co-founder and owner, added, "Along with Shad Heller and Peter Engler, Violet Hensley embodies the best of Silver Dollar City.

"Her love of life and dedication to her craft make her an unforgettable personality," he said. "No one is more loved or admired."

Similar sentiments ring out from Brad Thomas, Silver Dollar City general manager.

"Violet Hensley is an Ozark Mountain treasure," he said. "She loves people, she loves God, and she loves music. Her passion, her humor, and her talent of music and craftsmanship exemplify the true character that created the culture of the people of the Ozarks.

"I, and countless others, have all been blessed to have been hugged, entertained, and loved by Lady Violet," he said.

Though Silver Dollar City entertainment manager D.A. Callaway has known Violet for nearly 40 years, he focused his attention on her craft rather than her playing.

"I had never seen her in concert until this year (2012)," he said. "The several musicians in attendance were dumbfounded by her skills, knowledge of lyrics, melodies, fiddle tunings, and musical history."

Lisa Rau, Silver Dollar City publicity director, said one of her most memorable publicity trips in a 25-year career was with Violet in New York for "LIVE! with Regis and Kathie Lee."

"The evening before the show, we took Violet to a rock-n-roll sushi restaurant that she thought amusing," she said. "But the best part? Why the sushi came out on a beautiful platter. Violet looked at it, and looked again, rather puzzled, only to proclaim in quite a loud voice, 'Why that fish needs to go back into the creek!'

"Violet is an inspiration to those who seek to understand the heart and soul of Silver Dollar City — why it ticks like it does," she said. "Violet has always shown our guests her caring, genuine and humble personality that draws people into conversation … and then, she'll zing a funny, like dancing while playing the violin over her head!"

To learn more about Violet's Silver Dollar City home, visit www.silverdollarcity.com.

Randall Franks

As Silver Dollar City celebrated its 50th Anniversary in 2010, the City had Lindy Knight build a special hut near the front gate to house their Hall of Fame artisan and fiddler Violet Hensley. Her grandson Sterling Flagg works on a fiddle next to her.

Whittlin' and Fiddlin'
My Own Way

The wood upon which I was whittled

Folks often find their path in life already mapped out for them before the warmth of their Mama's arms quiets their first screams. If that was my parents' intentions, I bet I veered pretty far from whatever they had planned.

I don't know much about my birth on that cool 21st day of October in 1916 except it's possible that my Grandma Brumley stood by servin' as midwife for my Mama, Nora Elizabeth Springer Brumley. My father, George Washington or "Wash," and other kin probably waited anxiously by in the same log house where my father was born in 1874.

Speakin' of my family, my Grandpa, Joshua Brumley (1840–1908), came to Alamo, Arkansas from Tennessee and homesteaded buildin' that house. He met and married Rebecca Jane Crawford in Montgomery County, Arkansas. She had come to the Alamo Community from Georgia. They raised a family of 16 grounded in the fertile soil of the land. Grandma Rebecca, who was half Cherokee, was a midwife. I can remember folks often comin' to get her to bring new ones into the world.

My dad was 5 foot 3 inches tall. My Mama was that height too. Dad use to say they could put a board across their heads and put a bucket of water on it and they could walk without spillin' it. Dad was 36 and Mama was 24 when they got together. She came from Crystal Springs, Arkansas, though they lived at Alamo, after they married in October of 1910. Her folks — Francis M. and Mary Ann Standifer Springer — came from Standifer Gap, Tennessee. They both survived the effects the Civil War had on that area but decided to move further west after their marriage on December 22, 1866.

I came into a world at war. They called it "the war to end all wars" — though in my 97 years, the wars fought exceed the fingers on my hands. World War I did not really touch our family down in Alamo, but my dad once told me he was fixin' to have to go to fight when the war ended in 1918. The Spanish flu epidemic did come our way though. My dad's oldest brother died about that time.

The old log house where I was born sat on 90 acres that my dad farmed. There was a log shop and a smokehouse out behind it. I do not remember bein' in the log house at all, but I do still carry a scar given me there as I was crawlin' on the kitchen floor and got underfoot. Mama blundered over me and spilled hot gravy on my shoulder from the fryin' pan. Another time, according to some of our family tales, I was about 2 years old and had wondered where I shouldn't be. This time it was beneath the hooves of our horse, Womp. The horse started forward and Dad hollered "Whoa!" just in time. Womp put his foot back down straight rather than steppin' on me and instead just knocked me down.

I was third of four girls born to Mama and dad. The first was Dorothy Nell in 1912. Then came Emma Dee in 1914, but she was called home in three weeks. Finally, my youngest sister, Evaline, came along in 1918. I am sure my dad felt that he was outnumbered in that house as this passel of girls began growin' up. But on the farm, whether girl or boy, when you made your livin' from the dirt, it didn't matter how soft your hands were at birth — they would soon learn the meanin' of work and carry the calluses, scars, and toughness needed to turn dirt, water, and seed into a life for the family.

We all went to the fields to work. One of my earliest memories in the field was as I was lyin' at the end of the cornrows ringin' up rocks around me and watchin' while Dad and Mama hoed the corn. On one of those days, a little tortoise found its way to me and became one of the rocks I had around me. While watchin' my family work sometimes, I would tire with the rhythm of the hoes hittin' the earth and would float off to sleep. In my slumber, my little tortoise decided to find an escape from my play.

When I was 6 years old, Dad started me cuttin' grass away from the corn and choppin' cotton. We planted the cotton pretty thick, and you'd chop it and leave the plants about a foot apart. He often told me, "Violess, make yourself useful as well as ornamental."

By my sixth birthday, we had already come back from our year in Oklahoma. I guess with every generation, just like with my grandparents, there was an urge to go somewhere for greater opportunities — to better grass. Many of my uncles — John, Jack, and Will — and aunts — Adaline and Ellen — had chose Oklahoma as their new land of milk and honey. So when I was 5, Mama, Dad and my sisters and I climbed on board a train and traveled to Ada. Dad had packed his toolbox and two trunks and carried his fiddle with him on the train. I don't remember if the train took us all the way there, but I do remember the smoke billowin' from the smokestack of the engine. I remember the ding-dong of the bell and the choo-choo-choo-choo sound of wheels goin' round and round on the tracks beneath us.

When we changed trains in Hugo, we sat wait on the train platform, and Dad pulled out his fiddle to pass the time. I can still hear him playin' "Jericho" as the stationmaster and porters paused from their work to watch and listen.

I don't remember much about the trip to the new farm except the excitement of bein' in a new place. It didn't take us long to settle in and get to the work at hand. Before long, we started the same routines as we had in Arkansas — but we hoped this time we'd get better results.

My dad was enthusiastic as we began the first plantin' season. None of us could have known what was in store. Dad was in the field plowin' when he had a stroke. It hit so hard that before he knew it he was on the ground, and it was all he could do to crawl from the field to the house and call for Mama. We all came runnin' to him, and I am sure Mama was scared, not knowing what to do to help him. We got him into the house, and Mama sent Dorothy to Aunt Ellen's for help. Dad seemed like he was getting worse, but he was more concerned about Womp, so he sent Mama to unhook him from the plow and get the horse out of the field. She wasn't use to workin' with the horse, so Dad told me later she unbuckled the hames wrong, startin' with the top rather than the bottom and makin' the process difficult. Eventually, she rebuttoned them and started from the bottom.

I don't remember whether a doctor came, but before we knew much of what was to happen, Mama and us girls were sent off to stay with Mama's sister, Nellie Tennessee Springer, and her husband, Kelsey Hobby, in Tulsa. Dad stayed with his sister, Ellen, and Uncle Henry Davis in Ada. He always referred to his condition by sayin' he "couldn't move finger nor toe."

I remember ridin' in a mail hack to get there — changin' from hack to hack. It was about three feet wide and eight feet long. There was only a seat for the driver, so the four of us sat in the floor with the mail. On one of the hacks the driver had a spotted dog that rode along with us.

In a way, staying with Aunt Nellie was an adventure for us. It was a pretty big place compared to what we had seen. I had never been in a town before where the houses were close together. One day we walked to a little general store with Aunt Nellie, and someone we met there gave me the first money I guess I ever had in my hand. They handed me a nickel and said, "Go spend it." I bent over in the floor and spun it like a top. Everyone laughed. I don't know what I got with it.

After about a month, we heard that a country doctor had come by on horseback in Ada and gave Dad something that helped him get over the stroke. Before long we were all back together again on a train headed home to Alamo. Dad had his toolbox and his trunk and his fiddle, and I would have my next birthday back home. At least I thought I would be back home.

When we got back to Alamo, I learned the log house that we had left had burned down in our absence, so we took up housekeepin' at my Uncle Will's old log house that he left when he went west. It had a livin' room, kitchen, and two bedrooms — one off each room. It had a porch eighteen to twenty inches off the ground and was built around the well curb. There was a log smokehouse with a gooseberry bush next to it. I would pick those berries, and I loved them. We had a big old log barn, and we had a team of mules. It did not take us long to make Uncle Will's home our home, and us girls soon began findin' a little fun between our chores.

No matter what the season, we could find something that would keep us occupied. Remember that well on the porch I mentioned? We used a bucket to draw water out of the well, and my sister Evaline and I would sit on that bucket and lower each other down in that well and draw each other back out. We went to visit an old friend of my Dad's in 1986, McGrough (pronounced McGrew), who had boarded with Uncle Will. He told me that when they were diggin' the well with pick and shovel, a dog got after a sow and backed it off into the well. It didn't have water in it yet, but was deep enough that they had to get down in the well and put ropes around the hog and pull her out. It scares me now just to think of us girls lowerin' down into it. Evaline and I could be a bit darin' I guess. We would climb in the loft of the barn and jump out of it. It was high enough to drive a wagonload of cotton under.

Right under the hill from the house, there was a running creek. One winter it froze over. Evaline must have been 5 or 6 years old, and I must have been 7 or 8, and the water was over my dad's head. He said he heard us and come down there as I said aloud, "I heard it crack that time." We had gathered our skirts up and filled them with rocks and were throwin' them, tryin' to break the ice while standin' out on it. It scared us after he came and told us that if it cracked and we went through, he would have never known where we went.

Another thing happened when I was 6 — my first day at the Alamo School on 22 of August 1922. Of course, it would be hard to measure farm folks' time at school as a year. By the time I was 15, I had made it into seventh grade, and dad told my sisters and me we couldn't go any-more. He didn't have the money to buy us books. But while I was there, I did pick up quite a bit of learnin' and had a lot of fun with my friends Luda Driggers, Thema Jones, Lonetta Kinsey, and my sisters.

Alamo School was a one-room schoolhouse about two-and-a-half miles from our farm. All the grades met together. There was no outhouse at the school; the girls would go in the woods to one side and the boys on the other. We had a well and generally were lined up to get a drink out of the dipper before recess was done.

We walked to and from school each day that we went, but if it was too cold, or if we had work to do on the farm, our feet would not cross through the schoolhouse door. When we did go, we got up early and had breakfast and headed for the schoolhouse. We had to cross foot logs on the creek. If water was up, we had someway of goin' around it, over the mountain.

When I was in second grade, Lonetta Kinsey kept wantin' us to stay the night with her. Dorothy really wanted to, so one afternoon Dorothy and I decided to go home with her instead of goin' to our house. When we didn't come home, Dad went to our nearest neighbor, Wallace Cannon, who was Thema's stepdad. Thema told him where we were and he came to get us. It was about 11 p.m. when he got there. It seemed like I got a lick with the switch on one leg and then the other every time my foot hit the ground, but I know Dorothy felt the sting of it every bit as often as I did. That wasn't much fun, and we didn't ever try that again!

Through my years there we had several teachers — Joe Simpson; his sister, Miss Green; and Mr. Horn, who was let go for stealin' chickens.

Mr. Simpson was my first teacher and my last teacher. He was only 19 years old when I was in first grade, but my last year there he had two little girls that hung around me a lot. He always said I should be a school-teacher or run a nursery. I didn't turn out to be either one.

Spellin', readin', and writin' were my favorite subjects. Sometimes we would have a spellin' bee on a Friday and I would be the last or one of the last ones standin'. I guess I got that from my dad. You could give him about any word and he could spell it, but I never heard him read a word from a book. I always did his readin' for him.

One mornin' my last year, there was a buzz, buzz, buzz goin' on in the ceilin' of the schoolhouse, and every child was lookin' up. Since he had lost all the students' attention, Mr. Simpson said, "Big at each end, little in the middle; digs up dirt and, plays the fiddle." I knew what it was. Some of the kids didn't though. He had to tell them it was a dirt dauber buildin' a nest or dauber house.

One of my favorite times was recess. In one of our games we would take a pole and vault from one stump to another. We had stilts we would walk on. We'd play kick the can, hide and seek, baseball, flyin' Dutchman, anti over (also called Annie, Annie Over, or Andy Over, or Annie I Over), drop the handkerchief, and pop the whip. That was my favorite. In Pop the Whip ten or twelve kids would get in a line holdin' hands and the leader would run, takin' the "whip" as fast as they could until he or she would stop. You never knew when the leader was goin' to stop, usually causin' the whip to make kids pop off the end of the line.

In the fall we had to stay out and gather corn and pick cotton, peas, and beans. That was our food supply. We got to go to school a short time in August, at least the first few days, until corn gatherin' and cotton pickin' time. I never went regular. I may have gone in the wintertime a week without missin' a day. As I grew, the times at school were great fun, but my learnin' about how to live came mainly from our day-to-day efforts to keep food on the table, shoes on our feet, and clothes on our back. Those lessons have guided me well throughout my life and I hope that some of them rubbed off on my children and theirs after them.

Childhood games

Annie, Annie Over

1. Split the group into teams. Have half the kids go to one side of the house and the other half go to the other side.
2. Decide which team will go first by playing a rhyming game such as eenie meenie miney moe or one potato two potato.
3. Call out "Annie, Annie Over!" and throw the ball over the house..
4. Try to catch the ball as the ball comes over to your side. Throw the ball back over the house, and call out "Annie, Annie Over!" if you don't catch the ball.
5. Sneak around the house and throw the ball at members of the other team if you catch the ball.
6. You become a member of the other team if you are hit with the ball by someone on that team. If the ball doesn't hit a player, it's the other team's turn to throw the ball over.
7. End the game when one team has no more players.

Piggy Wants a Motion

Select a person to be the farmer. Everyone else is a pig. Designate an area to be a pig pen. The pigs then hide while the farmer looks for them. If he sees a pig, he yells, "Johnny, get in my pig pen." The caught pig then stands in the pen and says, "Piggy wants a motion." A pig in hiding can set the captured pig free by making a gesture. The pig in the pen then tries to escape without being seen by the farmer. Once all the pigs are caught, the game is over.

Kick the Can

Divide into two teams. One team will guard the can while the other team tries to kick it.

Violet's grandmother
Rebecca Jane (Crawford) Brumley

Violet's grandfather
Joshua Brumley

Violet's grandparents Frances and Mary (Standefer) Springer in about 1910

Joshua Brumley and John Brumley driving a
team of oxen in Hot Springs in 1890.

Violet's father George Washington
Brumley holds his fiddle on his farm in
Alamo, Arkansas in 1931.

Violet's mother
Nora Elizabeth Springer Brumley

The fields that sustained us

I don't doubt we'd've had everything we needed, except for flour, Dad's coffee, and a few other store-bought things from time to time. If we didn't have it, we made it. If it broke, we fixed it. If we ate it, we grew it. If we grew it, we kept enough seed from year to year to make our next crop.

Dad always got up at 4 a.m. and started a fire in the fireplace with pine splinters durin' the cold months. I still remember gettin' up early. I didn't mind it so much — it's not like I knew anything different. Most of the time I would race to the kitchen, climb up into a cane-back chair to grind dad's coffee. I always got a kick out of that. I loved my dad, and, even at an early age, I wanted to please him. He always had only one cup of coffee in the mornin'. If it happened to be too strong, sometimes he'd say "That's as strong as aquafortis (nitric oxide — pronounced, akifortus). Other times, he'd say "That's strong enough to float an iron wedge," or "That's strong enough to knock a mule down."

No matter what time of the year, there was always something for all of us to do. Bein' in the fields was just something we three girls thought was supposed to happen, and we all pulled our weight. We went to the fields to work together, usually by first light. The seasons would decide our tasks. Plantin' season would begin generally with clearin' and burnin' off a brush pile. That area would be the spot for Dad's tobacco to start. He liked to chew, but I never cared for it.

I hated to work in tobacco. The tobacco seeds are little tiny things, and we'd have to thin the plants out so they'd get big enough to transplant from there to his tobacco patch. As they growed those great big old leaves — eight or ten inches wide and two foot long — we'd have to top them. Under each leaf there'd be a sprout come out. They called them suckers. It wasn't that I hated the tobacco as a plant so much it was just all the stuff we had to do to it. You'd have to pick off the worms and pinch off the suckers every few days. When the tobacco got tall enough, we had to plow between the rows to kill the weeds. We went down one side of the row and up the opposite side with a two-footed plow, called a double shovel, that turned the dirt toward the plants.

After several hours of work in the fields, Dad could tell the time by lookin' at the sky, and he would send Mama in about 10 o'clock to get our noon meal prepared. We would head in to the house pretty near to noon for dinner. Though the years number near a century since those days, I can still smell my mother's biscuits hot from the oven as I neared the log house and stepped on the porch. My mom sure could cook, and nothin' made my mouth to water like her cakes, especially coconut. In the summer, dinner gave us a chance to cool a bit from the sun beatin' down on our backs as we tended the fields. Dad would sometimes take a rest in the heat of the day and sit in the shade of the house. He had a hickory bottom ladder-back chair that he had cut about an inch off the bottom of each leg. He'd lean back against the wall in that chair and fan himself with some small twigs with leaves tied together to create a breeze. He would often play his fiddle in the same chair at evenin' as us kids would be out playin' or climbin' trees.

After we got Dad's tobacco goin', we'd plant Irish potatoes and early garden vegetables like early English peas, onions, cabbage, radishes, and lettuce. We'd also bury, or cover, sweet potatoes in the dirt to grow slips or sprouts to transplant and grow. We also planted cotton each year, and one year we planted wheat. Usually, we'd plant a pumpkin hill or two among the corn. Once everything was in the ground we would get a short break from the fields until the little plants began stickin' their heads up. Then they needed cultivatin' until harvest.

I will never forget one time I was headin' to the tobacco patch with our mule, Cricket, and a young heifer hooked up to the plow. I just started out the gate of the barn lot across the road from the tobacco patch when Dad caught me and put a stop to it. He said, "You'll tear my tobacco patch all to pieces!" That was his exact words. A mule and a heifer will not pull together. That was the end of that. I had to unhook my team.

When we were not outside workin'; there was plenty to do inside. One of my chores was sweepin', and of course you couldn't sweep without something to move the dirt around. This was a situation where we grew to provide the tools we needed. So, we also grew our own broomcorn. When it began to seed, we would go along and break the stem over about four or five inches below the heads. We needed some of the stem to fasten the straw to the broom handle. Breakin' the stem over would allow the straw to grow down into great long straws about two feet long rather than bend over under the weight of the top and spread out like an umbrella. When the seeds were ripe we cut the tops off right where we had broken it over and took them to the scrub board and shelled the seeds off of it by pushin' the stem end downwards into the tub. You couldn't go the opposite direction because it would ruin the straw. Then we would take a few heads and make small bundles tied with string and hang them in the barn so they would stay straight.

I loved spendin' time with my dad watchin' him work, and I thought I could do anything he could do. I always wanted to do what he did just right. He trusted me to try it. One of those things was how to make a broom from the broomcorn. When one wore out, I would take the handle and get what I needed from the barn to make another. First I unwound the wire from the old worn-out broom, leavin' it tacked to the handle. Then I cut the stems about two-and-a-half or three inches long, leaving the stem part of the straw soakin' in water to soften so the wire could be wound tightly around it without cutting into the stem. I'd put the stems on the broom handle one at a time, rollin' the handle and windin' the wire over the top of them. After I placed one row of stems all around the handle with the straw hangin' down toward the floor, I was ready for the second row. This time I put three stems on one side and three on the other side with the straws turned up towards the top of the broom handle. The wire was wound over the stems, then the straw was turned down to form the shoulder. The ends of the straw were tied down to keep the straw from turnin' back up. Next, the third row was done like the first row with the wire wound all the way up from the shoulder to the top end of the stems and fastened to the handle with a tack. Then I took two boards and evenly flattened the straws between them about the middle of the length of what the broom straw would be when it was finished. I took two colors of coarse thread and tied four rows around the broom, alternatin' colors.

Next, I put one color of thread, say, red, in the broom needle. The broom needle was flat about 3/16 of an inch wide at the eye end and tapered to a point. The eye was about 1/16 of an inch wide and 3/8 of an inch long. The whole needle was about four inches long. Dad made it before I was born. I tied the red thread in the needle to the first row of strings around the broom. I put the needle down through the straw comin' out on the opposite side, and over the string around the broom on that side and back through the straw to the first side and back over again to draw the straw in tight. Each loop over the string around the straw was about half an inch apart all the way around. I did that to each of the four rows of string we had tied around the straw. Then took the boards off and trimmed the ends of the straw off straight across the bottom. Up until I got married, I don't remember ever buyin' a broom.

Another chore that I found myself doin' was washin'. As the old sayin' went, "Cleanliness is next to Godliness." We'd get a scrub board and get a bar of soap that we made to wash our clothes. First, we'd wet down the clothes and take the bar and rub it into the soiled spots. Then we'd put the soap into the holder on the scrub board and rub the clothes clean on the board. If you had a stubborn spot, you would have to take a second rubbin' with the soap. The process was a necessity for much of my life. Not until 1970 did I get my first washer and dryer.

We also used the same homemade soap to wash dishes. Dad taught me how to make the soap. He always made it by the light of the moon so the soap would not shrink up as bad. We made ours in an old iron wash pot with a fire under it out in the yard. First we'd boil three gallons of water and a can of lye together and stir that good with a wooden paddle. Then we'd put in five pounds of rendered hog fat and stir until it began to thicken. Once it started turning brown, it was almost done. The color of the grease determined what color the soap would be. We'd test it with a chicken feather. When it wouldn't cut the feathers off when you put it in the hot soap, it was done. It would smell like lye soap. We would pour it into a box to let it get harder, then cut it into squares about one-and-a-half inches thick, three inches wide and four inches long before we laid it out on a board. It would dry, shrink up, and stay hard, and you could store it in a bag. We used it for everything, includin' takin' a bath on Saturday and washin' our hair.

Back then we didn't have no bathtubs. We had a No. 3 washtub, and the whole family used it. Eventually we did get an oblong one shaped like a bathtub. You took a bath in by the cook stove or by the fireplace.

Usually, the youngest got first crack at it.

We got to go to school once the crops were in — that is, until harvest time came — and then we had to stay home to gather corn and pick cotton, peas, and beans. I liked goin' to school, and in a way I wished we didn't have to stop, but I loved spendin' the time workin' with my sisters as well. Even though I enjoyed the time with them, one thing I thought would never come to an end is pickin' beans. We planted so many beans and peas — black eyes, purple hulls, whippoorwill, crowder, and butter beans. We let them stay on the vine until they were dry, or we gathered them and let them dry on a sheet on a platform in the yard. We'd shell the beans and put 'em in cloth flour bags and put 'em away to eat for the winter. Sometimes I thought those beans would never end as we got them ready to store. When we needed some to cook, we would take out so many and remove all the bad ones — those that would have rotten lookin' spots or dried up pieces or any scrap pieces of hull — and wash and cook them.

One thing I never grew tired of was goin' out to the spot of peanuts when they came in. We would loosen them with a plow, pick them up, shake the dirt off and turn them towards the sun to let them dry before puttin' them in the barn. Before long, we were parchin' 'em in the oven and then makin' a mess droppin' the peanut shells all over the floor. Then I really would enjoy my work with my broom as I swept them shells into the fire.

The year we grew wheat I learned about usin' a wheat cradle — the five-fingered thing with a long blade that we'd swing. It had two hand-holds on it, and you used it to cut the wheat and it would land in it. Then you would put it up on your hip and bundle it. The bundle would be about as big around as my arm. We would tie a bundle of straw wheat around that and make it a bigger bundle, stack maybe a dozen of them bundles together, then lay some bundles over the top. We called it shockin' the wheat. It was sort of like when you made a corn shock — cuttin' the corn tops and bundlin' them in the field before going back later with the wagon to haul them to the barn loft.

Another part of harvest was pickin' fruit when it came in. We had peach and apple trees. By the time I was in my teens, we would dry peaches and apples. Eventually though, we moved on from the process of dryin' and borrowed a pressure cooker. We canned green beans and tomatoes as well.

I learned some great lessons that I would use throughout my life durin' these harvest seasons. Preparin' food to eat through the lean times was a great skill that served me and my family well.

I hate to admit it, but I was partial to sweet things. I loved walkin' the edge of the fields and along the roadsides with my bucket gatherin' blackberries. It would be a struggle to keep from emptyin' it as I walked. Thankfully, there was always another blackberry bramble to pull from. Probably the sweetest treat on the farm came from my dad's beehives. I loved workin' those hives with him. It was amazin' how much honey we could harvest, especially the year I married when he had 32 hives. We would also plant a spot with cane so we could have sorghum molasses. Though it was work, gatherin' to press the sorghum at the mill was sort of like a picnic. The mill was owned by one of the Powells — John Joe or Gilford. It was the only one in a neighborhood of four or five miles. They'd have to move it around from farm to farm. They'd move it to Lester Weston's place a quarter of mile from our place.

It took two mules to pull the mill. It went around in a circle, and the cane press would squeeze the cane and drain off the cane juice, something that looked like green water. We would load the cane in a wagon and all head over to the Weston's for the work. Once the press began, the juice would go into a vat that was twelve feet long, divided in sections. The process was fascinating, and I loved to walk along the vats. There were six of them things. As the liquid heated in the sorghum pan, it would form a green skim. The juices start in the first compartment where they let it cook a while, and then they would take out the rag that was used for a stopper and let the juice go into the next one and cook a while. The juice would continue through all the sections. The holes were on opposite sides of the divider in each compartment. In the meantime, new liquid was started in the first section and the process continued all day. We would stand by to skim each section. It got less green each time. It was just foam by the last section. We would skim the foam off and it would leave good sorghum molasses. For the last compartment, we would drain it out into a wash pot. When it was cooked off at the last cookin', I really liked eatin' the foam that you would skim off the sorghum. We kept it cookin' the whole time. We run off about 30 gallons, and that would last us all year.

We made Lester Weston's, Claude Hall's and our sorghum all at Lester Weston's place. On one of the many sorghum-millin' days, when I was 16, I was chose to change the teams on the mill at noon. I liked to handle the teams. I was good at it, and everyone knew it. Lester Weston's mules were black and red. I had seen the black one buck Lester off once. I turned our team loose and headed up the hill to get Lester's team. Jeff Norman, Claude's stepson, who was a year older than me, said, "Ride the black one, and lead the red." I guess he didn't think I'd do it. I bridled both mules and led them to a stump. I climbed on the stump and eased onto the black one. When I got up closer to the mill Jeff hollered, "Get off that mule, he'll kill you!" It wasn't no use to get off then, I was already there! In a way that reflected a lot of what was in store for me in life. I would step out on faith "knowin'" I would be safe, not realizin' what danger was potentially underfoot until it was passed.

Violet's Uncle Will, Uncle John and father, Wash Brumley

Violet Hensley's first day attending school in 1922.
She is the smallest child standing in the front row.

The good book and a new home

When I was a child, we weren't what you might call regular churchgo-
ers. That was probably because the nearest church was about a seven-mile
walk. Sometimes in the summer, we would get up early, I'd shave my
dad's face, and we would take off walking to Aunt Alice's house. Aunt
Alice was my dad's youngest sister, and her husband was Uncle Joe
Weston. He was a Baptist preacher.

If it was huckleberry pickin' time, we would often just stop along the
path and pick handfuls to eat as we went. If we planned ahead and
brought a bucket, we would fill it to make a pie later on. We also made
special trips to pick them for canning.

We went two or three times during the summer. Sometimes we rode
the wagon. In the summertime the wagon wheels would dry out, and we
would have to stop in the creek, fill a bucket, and pour water on the top to
swell the wheels up to keep the metal tires on.

When we'd walk we'd start in the morning and come back by dark,
starting out about eight o'clock on Sundays so we could get there before
services. You didn't have Sunday school like you do now. We met in a
plain one-room Missionary Baptist Church that looked like our schoolhouse. It was one open room with benches and windows along the sides
and a wood-burning heater stove to keep people warm. I liked to sit close
to the front. Unlike today, where folks tend to fill the back first and scat-

ter out, back then seats would start filling from the front and go towards the back.

How Uncle Joe started his services I don't remember, but he would stand up in the pulpit, start preachin' and just get louder. "I'm gonna get high now," he would say, and he'd begin talkin' louder and faster, preachin' 'bout what was gonna happen if you don't turn yourself over to God. "You got to let God into your life," he would say. Then he'd go into some Biblical point — don't lie to your neighbor, or whatever the lesson was about that day.

"What Would You Give in Exchange For Your Soul?" "When the Roll is Called Up Yonder," "Old Time Religion," "Farther Along," and "Amazing Grace" were some of the hymns we often sang.

Dad's teachings at home were simple, but they pretty much followed along with what I learned as I read the Bible to my Grandma Brumley. He used to say, "Treat your neighbor as you wish to be treated," and "If you are a neighbor, you will have a neighbor; if you are a friend, you will have a friend." Dad often repeated a story about a stranger coming into the neighborhood wanting to know about the neighbors. The stranger asked, "How were the neighbors where you are from?" If people told him they had good neighbors in their hometowns, he knew they'd be good neighbors also. If they said they had bad neighbors, he knew he could expect to find them the same way.

Even when we didn't attend church services, Dad always tried to keep Sunday as God's day of rest. We'd usually spend the day around the farm or sometimes walk to a neighbor's house. Resting would sometimes mean a little bit of play for us, too. A swimmin' hole by Wallace Cannon's place on the creek was one of our favorite summer Sunday pastimes, as it was for other nearby families. My dad always wore overalls, and when the knees in his overalls would wear out, he'd cut 'em off for swimmin'. He could really swim. Us girls would wear his old cut off overalls. I would wade the creek but I never tried hard enough to learn to swim.

When I was eleven, two things changed our lives dramatically. First, was we moved into our new two-room house that dad built along with help from me and the other girls. We had lived at Uncle Will's for about five years before it was finished. I helped make and put shingles on that new house. We'd take mud soil and roll it out like a pie crust then put crab grass in it. Starting at the edge of the circle, we would roll it up so that it got bigger in the middle and pointed outward at each end, completely hiding the grass. The grass held it all together.

We'd build the fireplace up to the hips with rocks and used mud to dob them in, sealing the rocks. Then we had two-by-fours or four-by-fours on up past the top of the house with strips nailed on them cross-ways. We wrapped these "mud cats" over, joining each cat agin the other so there was no space showing between. The chimney was dirt and grass from the hips to the top of the house.

We were so excited to move in to the new house, because we had a hand in making it. There is so much energy that comes from having somethin' new that you helped to make with your own two hands. Despite the enthusiasm, it wasn't long until we were back into the day-to-day existence of survival and caressing the earth to give us what we needed. As a child, I knew I got tired, but it was not until the second thing that changed our lives came that I realized how that tiredness could turn into stillness.

It was another day in the fields for all of us except Mama when the death angel came and took her away. Today, I don't really remember much about her except that she made our clothes. She never wore a short dress or cut her dark black hair. She always wore her hair done up in a bun on the back of her head. I had a couple of her dresses for a long time. They were so small — she was very small around the waist. I sometimes think if she had lived there might have been a few more feminine ways mixed into my sisters and me.

She took sick with what was likely the flu. Not well enough to come to the fields, she stayed home and did the cookin'. When we came in at the end of the day from workin', she was layin' on the bed. Dad asked, "Nora, Is supper ready?" and she said, "Aw, yes, all but the bread." She started to get up to tend to it, but she didn't have the strength. She fell deep back into the pillow. She couldn't take on any nourishment herself, and before long we were sent to bed. I guess my dad sat up with her that night 'cause he roused us early and sent Dorothy and I out on foot to go for the doctor. We hadn't made it far, just down to the little creek we had to cross, until we heard him calling us back home. That was the longest walk I think I had ever taken as we made our way back. Somehow I knew at the end of it, my mother would no longer be there, I would never hear her voice again, never eat one of her wonderfully prepared cakes. Dad sent my sisters and I to let the neighbors know that Mama was gone.

My dad and someone else built a small wooden coffin, and Myrtle Cannon and Mantha Pettitt came and lined it with a white satin. They took the bed out of the room and prepared a platform in the middle that the coffin sat on overnight. Neighbors came by to see her, and many set up with her through the night. The next morning, we headed for Peak Cemetery in Meyer Creek. I reckon they went on horseback to spread the word. My Uncle Roland Moore in Crystal Springs got there with his Model T truck. They loaded the box on the back of a truck up towards the front. We all sat around it as we traveled the seven or eight miles to the cemetery.

Quite a few people were there when we arrived. The menfolks dug the grave with picks and shovels. Everyone lined up around the grave. Tears filled all our eyes as they lowered the coffin and the menfolk covered it up with shovels of dirt. We got back on the truck and went home, and that was that. Not like today, no songs, no pretty words, just we that cared, standing around looking down at her eternal resting place.

The next day after the burial, Dad burned sulfur in the house and gave the bedding some kind of treatment. I remember that smell so well. It was to get the sickness out of the house. As I looked into my dad's face, I could see that he was so sad, the lines in his forehead and cheeks seemed deeper than they ever had before. The worry of what was next I know hung heavy in his heart as he looked into the faces of his daughters — ages nine, eleven and fifteen. It wouldn't take long until he would have to force himself back out into the fields.

About nine days later, Dad had his hands full again worried that he would lose all us little ones. Our cousin Harvey Moore was at the funeral — and he was carrying the measles. We all got them. Since medical care was not the norm in our neck of the woods, he had to do his best to tend to the farm in May, along with us, as the fevers, sore throats, and the rash came and thankfully went without taking any of us to join Mama. It wasn't Dorothy's first bout with sickness. She was not as much a tomboy as my younger sister and me. She was more ladylike. She had an awful tough time as a little girl getting spinal meningitis when she was about two. Dad said she bent over all the way backwards, and her head touched the back of her feet. He bought peppermint candy by the shoebox-full to feed her during her illness. Aunt Martha, who lived in Hot Springs, took her awhile and cared for her. She had to learn how to walk all over again at age three. Despite that experience, she grew up and worked hard like we did.

After we were well from the measles, we hardly missed a day of planting, tending, or harvesting without doing some kind of work in the fields. Dad didn't work on Sunday except this year 'cause it was too wet and we had no choice if we wanted to eat. We figured God would understand. He was the one that sent all the rain. Dad amazed me at all the work he did. He used to say, "I have one foot in the grave and the other on the ground." My dad worked so hard. Sometimes I think his body wore out long before it should have. No matter what he faced, he kept working, and he shared with us the wisdom that life had taught him.

I didn't realize until I experienced some of the aches and pains of life what he really must have went through. He had a bad hip, but he still had to farm. There was no welfare, no Social Security back then. With Mama gone, we all had to do a little more around the house. When Dorothy turned 16, she was our main cook and housekeeper. We had to start making our own beds and helping out. Dad did a lot of cooking. When we went home from the field, my oldest sister was sent to the house to make the noon meal. I was about 12 years old when I started cutting my dad's hair and shaving him. As I did, I remember how his blue eyes would sparkle when the light hit them as I was cutting away. He wore a hat most of the time, but of course that would come off revealing that he was bald on top and had a strip of black hair around the sides that never turned gray that I remember.

Outnumbered three to one, Dad sure had the disadvantage as the three of us grew and him without a woman around to help us along into womanhood. When I was 14 my Grandma Rebecca moved in with us. By that time though, she was not able to move around much or even get up. She was a heavy lady, and us girls had to help her up and down. She was not able to walk by herself. She would just sit in a chair on on the edge of the bed. She was a lot of fun though and liked to kid with us, especially when we were younger. Before she lived with us, she used to take her false teeth lower plate and kinda stick them out at us. It would scare me, and I remember running away from her. She thought it was funny.

When she lived with us, I am sure my youngest sister and me aggravated her when Dad wasn't looking. She would get after us with her walking cane. She would stick the end of it in the fire, and then she would take it like she was gonna burn us and we would get out of the way. She could only reach toward us. She couldn't get out of the chair. She wouldn't really have stuck it to us. We all thought it was funny. I still remember they put her in a wagon in a regular straight chair and hauled her up to the neighbor's house, which was a quarter mile from us, and she delivered a baby for Claude and Nette Hall on my fifteenth birthday. They named their baby girl, Viola, after me. I guess they would have taken

Grandma to the Hall's house in Grandma's Model T car if someone could have driven it. Dad tried it once, but when it tried to climb the plum tree, he got out and never tried again. All his life he only drove oxen, mules, or horses. When I was 15 Grandma moved back with Aunt Martha. She died three years later at 96.

While everyone worked hard in those days, without the medical advances and the financial props provided by the government we see today, the loss of a loved one came and went, and we had to keep working. Every day we kept working — sad, happy, cold, hungry, we had to keep working. The animals had to be fed, the crops had to be tended. That made the difference as to whether we would stay on this side of the dirt or join our loved ones in eternal sleep.

Did I miss my mother as I grew up? Yes, today I think I miss her more because after years of being a mother and grandmother myself, I would have welcomed her thoughts, her prayers and being able to share with her my many life experiences that I hope she would be proud to have seen me do. One day I will join her and Dad, and my kids and grandkids will gather 'round my casket lined with satin, and I will know not what they will face ahead. Just as I stood and looked down into Mama's grave, they will do so with mine. Just as my mother left her love in my heart and the strength to face the work ahead within my soul, I do the same for them knowing that if they wish to thrive and succeed, they can and they will. I did that for her, they should do no less for me. Each of us carries within us the hopes and dreams of all that came before us. I pray they have the strength to carry on all my dreams for them.

Violet Hensley's homeplace

Dad's fiddles and learnin' to play

The handyman of the community, Dad repaired sewing machines, plows, and fiddles. People would bring him plows to sharpen in his little blacksmith shop that consisted of a furnace and an anvil. During much of his free time, he made fiddles, a craft he inadvertently learned from his older brother, Sam — not that Sam intentionally did the teaching. See, there were three boys older than my dad — Uncle Sam, Uncle Jody, and Uncle John; and Dad had a twin named James Jackson known as Jack. Uncle Sam was in his twenties in 1888, when Dad was fourteen, and Sam had a fiddle he had played for ages. Dad wanted to play it too, but Sam wouldn't let him. "Somebody made 'em," Dad said at the time, "and I can, too." Dad decided to figure it out and ended up making his own instrument. I don't know how he managed it. He nailed nails in a board to bend his first sides. Then he decided to make what he called a rim press.

Dad didn't number his fiddles. For some of them, he wrote right on the inside wood with a pencil "Made by G.W. Brumley" right there on the back of the fiddle before he put the top on. There is no way of knowing how many he made. I imagine he made three or four a year. He always said he'd make one in about three weeks, working at it pretty steady, usually in wintertime while sitting by the fireplace. If he started one, he pretty well kept on it until he got it done. At that time, you would sell a fiddle for a dollar, although I don't really remember him getting cash for a fiddle. It usually was a trade. He'd make one and get a cow and calf in return. Somebody offered him a bull cow for one and he didn't need it, so he didn't trade. One time he traded his work for some old wagon parts to rebuild another one from the parts of the two of them. He traded another for a shotgun and another for some corn to help us through the winter.

As far back as I could remember I would want to help. By the time we girls were big enough to pull the end of a saw or use an ax, we were helping hands. If we wanted to learn anything he would let us try. I remember I couldn't be more than six years old and I'd say, "Shoot, I can make one of them fiddles." Then I'd run and hide. I didn't start making the instruments until I was 15.

I copied my rim press from his, only making it smaller. I just took a page, probably from an old Sears and Roebuck or Montgomery Ward catalog, folded it in half, and cut out my pattern. I didn't know it then, but it was a 1/16th size. He didn't exactly teach me how to make the fiddle. I just observed as I helped him cut the wood and listened at him talk. I had the advantage of him. I knew how he was working on them. I knew how he bent his sides. I knew how he thinned them. I knew how he talked about how thin to make the backs and the tops, how he glued them together. I helped him put clamps on. We cut a C shape in a block of wood for a clamp. So I had the advantage of him there. I wanted no help, and that was was my attitude. He made them without any help, and I imagine he made a few mistakes.

I finished my first fiddle in 1932. Times were poor then, and often we didn't have anything extra, but we got by. I turned 15 in October that year, and I made the fiddle in February, putting the date on the fiddle. I made three more fiddles between February 1932 and August 1934. The second fiddle was full size, and I gave it to my Dad's twin brother, Jack. The third was another 1/16th size, and Luda Driggers traded a quilt she made for it. I hung onto my number four fiddle, and that's the one I play. I used a pencil and drew four flowers on the top —one on either side of the fingerboard and tailpiece. Then I drew four more the same on the back and added a flower in the center back. Using red, yellow, and green crepe paper, I wet the tip of each one and painted the leaves green and the flowers red and yellow. I also used a pencil and drew purfling around the edge instead of inlaying real purfling.

Of course, I just didn't want to make them; I wanted to play them too. My dad was a fiddler of a sort, but he didn't play like I do. As I look back now, I know Dad wasn't one of the best fiddlers. He had a rough approach and used simple fingerings, but he had good timing and a rough mastery of the bow that gave him a good feel for square dances. I learned some of my best music like "Waltz of the Violets" from Uncle Jim Pettitt. He had a smooth, fluid sound to his fiddle and put in more notes than my dad. I would say if compared with a popular fiddler he would be like Tommy Jackson. Uncle Jim lived three to four miles west and he would come and stay with us and help work for a few days in the summer. Him and my dad was good friends but not related. He lost his wife and lived alone but would come down to visit us. Whenever I shaved Dad on Sundays, I'd shave Uncle Jim too if he was there. I learned "Fire on the Mountain," "Sweet Bunch of Daisies," "After the Ball," "Tom and Jerry," "Durang's Hornpipe," and many tunes from Uncle Jim.

Sam Moore was another fiddler and a neighbor that lived the other direction from us. His style was more like my dad's — playing fewer notes in the tunes — and they both played for square dances. I play a tune I call the "Sam Moore Waltz" that I learned from him. I forgot the real name of the tune. I also learned from my Uncle Jack Brumley, dad's twin brother, and I still play a song I call "Uncle Jack's Tune" because I can't remember the original title.

My fiddlin' all started with the tune "Rose Nell" that my dad played. I just picked it up. Best I remember, the tune just rang in my head. I could whistle it while I worked in the fields. Of course, when my mother heard me she would say, "A whistlin' woman and a crowin' hen never come to no good end." That didn't slow my whistlin' though. The more I whistled, the more I thought I could play, and one day I picked up Dad's fiddle. I don't remember him showing me a note. It just came so natural. Once I'd heard someone play a tune, I could pick it out on the fiddle.

Dad would sit by the fireplace and play, sometimes with Uncle Jim or Sam, and Dad would hand the fiddle to me, and I would give the tune a try like "Billy in Lowground," "Sally Johnson" or "Leather Britches." Occasionally I would miss a note. When I knew it was wrong, I'd draw the bow across the strings real hard and start over again. Then he or Uncle Jim would show me how it went. There wasn't much time for prac- tice in those early days, but I did pick it up every chance I had. When we came out of the fields and finished our evening chores such as carrying water or wood and caring for the animals, only then could I play a little. This actually set up a practice approach that I would use later in life. When I was learning a new tune, I would play it before going to bed, and that tune would go over and over in my mind as I drifted to sleep. The songs just stuck in my head better that way.

When the weather was warm, we sat on the porch and played, hearing the neighbors from a quarter mile away yell out, "Play the Eighth of January!" While I thought fiddlin' came naturally, I guess the hardest part was matching the combination of bowing in time with the fingerings. I don't read music. I play strictly by ear. I remember playing for square dances along with my dad by the time I was 13. People would come to our house on Saturday night, visit Wallace Cannon's house another Saturday night, and then go to John Joe Powell's the next time. There wasn't a set house. Since people usually didn't have anything but a bed in their bedroom — no chest of drawers or anything like that — we would simply put the mattress in another room where visitors with babies put the little ones to sleep. We would usually start right after dark most of time in winter, and we would end up about midnight depending on how big a crowd we had. Everyone ate at home, so there was no food for the occasion, just music.

Often, six or seven couples would be there. You could not have a square dance unless you had at least four couples. The musicians would be over in one corner of the room. Some folks would be standin' 'round the wall, and they would change partners. I can't remember all the calls, but they had one they called the Grapevine Twist. Now, that was a tangled up one! The arms joined, and you would step over the arms. I can remember us being all lined up, and we'd turn around and step over the arms. I remember Wallace Cannon doin' some calling', sayin', "The bird hops out and the crow hops in." Another started out, "All hands up and spread out wide," and you would circle right and then circle left. The caller would say, "Swing your neighbor, now swing your own," and "do si do." I don't remember any other fiddler a-playin' there unless it was Sam Moore. He was the only other square dance fiddler in the neighborhood.

One dance set would last until each couple went through the routine of the call. Occasionally, we might have a drifter through. We had a couple men one time. I don't know where they were from or where they went, but they stayed at our house two or three days and drifted on. They didn't even go to the field with us. We had a couple of plum trees, and they just stayed out in the yard on a quilt under those trees in the day and then slept on the porch. One of them played the fiddle. The other one did a thing in his throat that sounded like a gurgle, like blowing a jug. I could never mock the sounds he made. They did a tune called the "St. Louis Blues" that I learned to play. I know they played several more. I musta been about 14.

That was just the beginning of my learnin'. When I started performing later in life, I would practice a little at home or do tunes at a jam session. Sometimes I would play by myself. If my husband Adren was off from work, sometimes he played guitar with me. I have learned throughout my musical life. Every fiddler I have ever met has given me somethin' to listen to. Sometimes it's been somethin' that I liked and tried, and sometimes it has been somethin' I didn't, and I left it on his or her fingerboard for someone else to admire. I learned tunes such as "Ragtime Annie" and "Lost Indian" since I started working at Silver Dollar City. I've always loved listenin' to fiddle music on radio and records. Some of my favorite fiddlers were the Kessinger Brothers, Tommy Jackson, and Mac Magaha. Some have asked me to describe my sound. Well, its old time fiddlin' just like we have had here in Arkansas throughout my life. I would say I play similar to Tillman Pyatt, or Dean Johnson and Lonnie Roberts. I hope that I get more of a sweet, listenable sound because I have worked to have a nice touch with the bow.

Most audiences I have performed for are real cheerful. Many times they will start clapping when they see me walk to the microphone. At this point in my life, it's probably just my age — they are just amazed I am still around. Even forty years ago in Washington, the roar of the thousands of people there when I stepped up on stage still rings in my ears. They were so far back they looked like specks. I was nervous, but I just tried to set the fiddle just right so they could hear it good and laid into "Soldier's Joy." We didn't talk there, we just played. I have never really been a talker on stage. I might name the tune or introduce my musicians, but I let the music do the talkin'. Unlike back when I started, today I just go out there and I don't worry about making a mistake at all. If I start off in the wrong direction, I just stop, say, "Woops, wrong tune," smile real big at the audience, and get after it again. It usually yields a ripple of laughter.

My life would be pretty dull without music. If I'm tired and play it, it soothes and relaxes me. It puts hope in my heart, a spring in my step and makes my feet want to dance. That is what I try to share with audiences each time I step on stage. I try to reach the tips of their toes with my notes. I want to see them moving with the music and watch that bubble up within them as it reaches their face and breaks into a smile.

Above: Three of Wash Brumley's fiddles. Below: Wash Brumley's tools currently on display at the Heritage House Museum of Montgomery County, Arkansas.

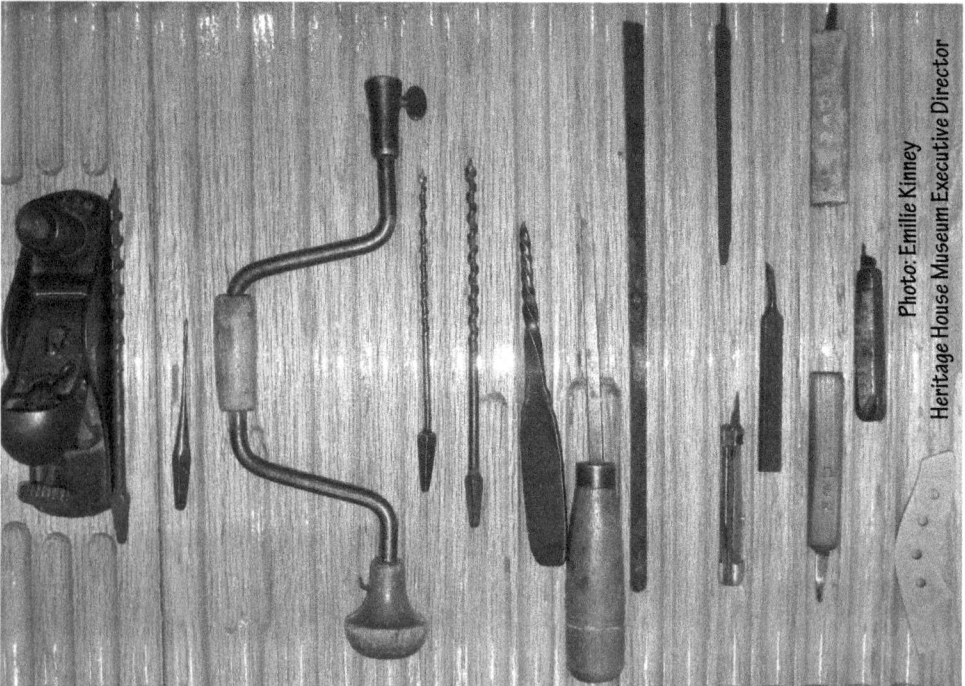

Photo: Emilie Kinney
Heritage House Museum Executive Director

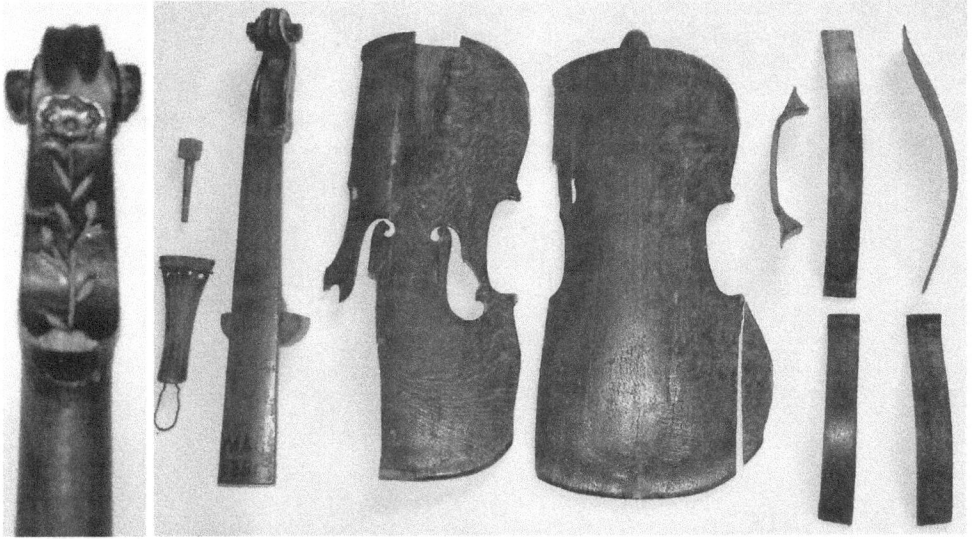

Violet Brumley made this fiddle at age 15. It was destroyed in the 1940s.

Evaline Peden, Wash Brumley holding Beatrice
and Marvin Hensley, and Violet in 1938.

Grab a root and growl

My dad would always say, "Grab a root and growl." That was his way to let us know we needed to get back to work after takin' a break. Work was one thing that came in never-endin' supply on the farm, and that did not change much as the cold weather came on.

The smell of new shoes is somethin' we only experienced once a year as the cold began to nip at our toes. My dad plowed barefooted in the summer, and so did I. I so looked for'ed to gettin' new shoes. When I was ten, I got a pair of button high top shoes. They were the only pair like that I ever owned. The rest were lace-ups. My Aunt Martha would bring out her old shoes and leave them with us, and we girls would tramp around in them for fun, but we never wore those away from the farm. As the cold season came close to its end and warm weather came on, we'd fix the wore out soles usin' a shoe last, and a half sole and we'd put on new heels.

As the 1920s came to a close, we heard there were lots of folks walkin' around with wore out soles on their feet and tired souls in their body after a big stock market crash in 1929. I was told from the second-hand newspapers dad would get that for some folks things were so bad they would jump right out the windows of a big tall buildin' in the big cities. Other than the talk of the older folks though, I don't remember any of us girls payin' any attention to what eventually pushed the country into the Great Depression and put millions into soup lines and into losin' their homes.

I didn't learn much about all of that until I was much older, because things didn't really change that much for us. Work was still the same, day in and day out. I remember Dad talkin' about how prices were goin' up. My dad didn't have no money in the banks, so the bank closures didn't hit us. We didn't have anything to do with no banks. We just lived day-to-day on the farm.

When the weather turned colder, it was time to kill hogs. Even though we depended upon our animals for survival, I was about nine years old when I saw my dad knock a hog in the head with a sledgehammer. I remember feelin' so sorry for it, but I knew from that hog's sufferin' we would have meat to eat. We had a pin to station the hog in and a place between the house and the barn where we would butcher the animal. Dad would do it when the weather was cold enough in November and the moon was dark and growin' towards the light.

We smoked the ham and shoulders and buried the rest, includin' the feet, backbones, ribs, and middlin' in salt in a saltbox. The middlin' was the part you make bacon from, but we didn't make bacon out of it. You just dug the salt away and cut a chunk of meat off, and you'd have to soak it awhile to get some of the salt out before we cooked it. We sliced the middlin's and fried it for breakfast or put a chunk in a pot of beans. The backbone was good for boilin' in beans. We boiled the pigs feet after the hoof was removed, and while we liked it, it had lots of bones. The head was used to make souse meat the day we butchered or the next day. I don't remember exactly how we made it except that after the hair was scraped off and eyes, nose, ears, tongue, and brains were removed, we boiled the head and picked off all the meat. We used as little water as possible, and the meat and broth jelled together. We never skinned a hog. The hog was put in a barrel of boilin' water to loosen the hair. Then we took it out and scraped it. The skin was cooked with the meat. The entrails were put in a tub, and we took the fat off and rendered it to make soap with. That was the job that my sister Evaline and me usually did. I had to be so careful not to break the entrails and ruin the fat. We boiled the tongue. The entrails and other remains were used to feed the dogs. We usually gave two neighbors a fresh mess of meat — usually the liver and brains — and sometimes a piece of the ribs. They usually did the same for us. The cows even got in on it, because they licked the wall of the house where the salt would seep through and make the boards salty. Dad never threw anythin' away but the hooves, hair, and the squeal.

As the winter wore on, we would continue preparin' things we would use through the rest of the year. One I really liked a lot was tannin' leather 'cause I knew come spring I would have a new bean flip to shoot with. A bean flip is also called a bean shooter or a slingshot. We'd use big beans or small rocks in them to shoot. But before I had the pleasure of shootin' a walnut or hickory nut out of the tree with my bean flip, we had to tan a calf hide to get a piece of leather to make it.

Us girls helped Dad tan the leather. First we put it in a stone crock with ashes and water until the hair was ready to slip off easy. Then we took it to the creek and washed all the hair off. Next, we made a tannin' trough out of about a three-foot-long hollow oak log we split in half, using one of the halves for the trough. We cleaned it out and nailed a board to each end, put the hide in, and filled it with water and pieces of red oak bark. We soaked it until the hide was stained brown. Then we washed it in the creek again. Two or three of us workin' at the same time would start squeezin' the water out by takin' a hold of the hide and pullin' that spot back and forth with our hands. As we squeezed, we began to work the oil in. That made a nice, pliable piece of leather, which we used for shoelaces, mendin' harnesses, and anything else we needed leather for.

Sittin' up agin one wall of our house was a black pedal Singer sewin' machine that I had watched my mother use as she made the clothes that we wore. Now my father used it to sew. I watched him each time he took up some project on it, tryin' to see how it was done. I knew I wanted to know how to sew. I had only two dresses, and I wanted another when I was 13. For my first one, I made it like a pillowcase from reddish brown material with a neck in the top and armholes in each corner. It didn't fit too well, but I wore it. After that, I learned to sew well enough that I was sewin' for the neighbors before I married. They'd look at pictures in the catalog and pick the dress they wanted. I'd take measurements and make a pattern out of newspapers. Later in life, I would use some store-bought patterns. With each new task I took on and completed, I guess I felt I was that much closer to bein' grown and able to take care of others.

With the spring came the beginnin' of the growin' of our food, and we would be out behind the mule sayin' "gee" to get it to go right and "haw" for left while we prepared the fields. It was also time for us to purify our blood with dark sassafras tea made from diggin' up the roots of the plant. We would use Doan's Little Liver Pills and Black Drought for any type of constipation.

But even those treatments would not help me the year our school got its first school bus. The bus was just a truck with a bed and sideboards and a bench on either side of the bed for us kids to sit on. As I stood up from the bench, my side started hurtin' as we got off the bus at Iley Pettitt's. I was all doubled over as we climbed the half-mile over the mountain to our house. Dad got Dr. Stewart from Norman, and he put a turpentine stoop — a cloth soaked in turpentine — on my side, sayin' I had appendicitis. I was so sick, but my dad nursed me through it. I was in bed seven weeks. Durin' that time, my food was the water off of cooked rice or cooked oatmeal. I was not allowed any of the grain. They also gave me doses of castor oil. One time I was eatin' my rice water and a drop of castor oil got in my food and I couldn't eat a bite of rice for years after that. I don't remember thinkin' about how bad I was; I just hated the medicine I had to take. By the fourth week, I was able to move around a bit. I got so skinny that the skin on my arms got flabby enough I could hold my arm up and wrap the skin around it. Dr. Stewart called me "plug ugly" and said if I fell in a creek, tell my boyfriend to look up the creek for me. I guess he thought I was light enough to float upstream.

Once I was up and goin' again, I was back to my usual tomboy activities. Huntin' and fishin' got a lot of our meat except for a few animals we would raise and butcher. My sisters and me would trap with dad — catchin' skunks, possums, and even a few coons. The skunks and possums brought about ten cents if skinned properly, and a coonskin would bring fifty cents to a dollar.

While to some folks our existence may have seemed monotonous, for us each new day brought somethin' new. Maybe it would simply be a visit by some kinfolks. Aunt Martha had some boys — Josh and Lawson McBride. They would come by up from Hot Springs to go huntin' or fishin' with my dad. In the summer, they helped in the fields so dad would take off and go fishin'. Huntin' was in the fall and winter for squirrels. We raised our own chickens and would kill one when kinfolks came on Sunday. One Sunday I remember some of Aunt Annie Moore's folks were there, as were Josh and Lawson. The boys had been fishin' and caught the soft-shell turtle. They cleaned it on the porch, and we sent it to the kitchen for mother and the aunts to cook. "Boys will be boys," I often heard, and in that form Lawson picked up the now-severed head of that old turtle remarkin' "Watch it bite Josh," as he stuck it to his arm. Sure enough, it did grab hold of Josh's arm — and it left a scar shaped like its teeth there. He carried it until he was killed a couple of years later at a dance at the age of 19. That's when I learned well that just 'cause you cut somethin's head off doesn't mean it won't hurt you.

We often enjoyed havin' people stop by, and if it was someone that my Dad really liked, as they would leave, dad would stand in the door, rub his hands together, rub his face and he would say, "Aye God, there goes some good people." One day in July of 1934, Evaline and I went to the field to pick a bucket of green peas to get somethin' to cook for lunch. We met these two boys along the path down by our barn. They were Adren Hensley and Ezra Hall. I don't remember if we even said "hi" because I was so shy. I wouldn't even look at anybody hardly. We just kept walkin' on to the field. I told Evaline out of their earshot, "The brown-eyed one's mine, even if I never get him." We got back to the house, and the boys were there talkin' with Dad. They stayed there a while and went on their way. Adren then started comin' by a week or two later. He would sit around and talk with dad. Dad would play the fiddle some. I would play the fiddle some, too. We never went on a date nowhere.

Adren usually brought another boy with him, and when it was time for us to go after the cows, they would walk with us over to the road, as we walked to the woods to listen for the cowbells so we could bring in the cows. We usually milked the cow from when she had a calf in February or March until fall. Then she would slack up until she had another calf the next year. The cows would lie out all night after the calves got big enough to eat grass, if we didn't bring them in.

Adren was footloose at 15 because his mother, Savannah, had died of the flu. His father, Dave, had died of malaria when Adren was seven. Their family was already livin' near Sobol, Oklahoma. They had migrated originally from Hohenwald, Tennessee, to Montgomery County, Arkansas, where Adren was born, and then on to Oklahoma. Savannah remarried James Pate sometime after that. Adren's brothers and sisters were Arthur "Ott," Oscar, Fred, George, Ella Mae, Sally Ann, Daisy, Christine, and Aline Pate. Woodrow and Drewey were his brothers that died as infants. Bein' the youngest boy, most of his siblin's were out and married on their own except Fred and George, when he was orphaned. They did some cuttin' timber and sellin' it, and he worked for a man makin' moonshine. After his mother died, Adren would stay here a while and there a while with different relatives and friends. He was just a lonesome, ramblin'-around boy. He had the attitude that he didn't want to be bossed.

A lot of young people around that time in our area didn't have a place of their own. They lived off their mamas and dads, or grandmas and grandpas. Since Adren was orphaned except for a stepdad that he didn't see eye-to-eye with, he went away hoboin' on the freight trains and hitch-hikin'. He told me he had hitched on top of a train one time and even rode between the cars on the couplin'. He would hide inside empty box-cars as he rode the train cross-country. Sometimes, he told stories of him and one of his friends as they were hoboin' gettin' off the train in small towns to ask for food or gettin' rousted off the train by railroad yard security in Hugo, Oklahoma. I wish I had remembered those, but they were a world away from our lives together and I didn't really want to know about them.

Even after we met, the desire for hoboin' was still inside of him. It took him away for several months, and he didn't even write. At that time, we really weren't considered boyfriend and girlfriend, but I didn't know that much about that kind of thing. Eventually he came back and stayed with folks in Ragweed Valley. He walked sixteen to seventeen miles to be at our house by noon on Sunday. I knew they had to get up early to be there to have lunch with us, and then they left later in the evenin'. He came every Sunday for quite a while. One Sunday he brought his wid-owed stepdad, Jim Pate, and eventually Jim married my older sister, Dorothy. He said he was forty, and acted forty, but we found out later he was really the same age as my dad, sixty years old. Dorothy was only 24. They had thirty years together, and raised seven kids. After Dorothy and Jim got married, Adren would come by himself and sometimes on Saturday would spend the night in our back bedroom.

Late April one Sunday mornin' we rose about 5 a.m., and I got break-fast ready for everyone. Dad and I were already seated at the table, and I went to the door and hollered for Adren, "Breakfast is ready!" He woke up, and I was still standin' at the door. He looked up at me and mumbled with his dark brown eyes shinin' at me. "I'm awake." As I looked in his eyes from the door, he continued to speak, sayin', "Will you marry me?" He wasn't speakin' loud enough for my dad to hear what he said. I didn't hesitate a bit. Before he could blink his brown eyes, I said, "Yes."

I went back to the kitchen, and he joined us shortly. It was very quiet around the table, and finally Adren mustered the courage to tell my dad, "Me and Violet is gettin' married." Dad drew a long breath, leaned back in his chair, and sighed while lookin' at us both. He didn't say anythin', but soon a smile came on his face, and as he finished breakfast, he said, "Well, get these dishes done up Violess. We got to get to the field." My dad was pleased because he thought he was gettin' someone to work on the farm. I never dreamed that one little word "yes" would begin the next sixty-two years together.

At that time, Adren was stayin' with his uncles and aunts and some with his sister Daisy "Dell" and her husband Clifford Pate. He was with Daisy at the time we got married as best I recall. My sister Evaline had married the week before to Lester Peden, one of the boys that was comin' up with Adren on Sundays. Lester was there more than Adren. Evaline and he would stand out by the plum bush. One day, I decided I was goin' to aggravate them a bit, and as I was up to my mischief my foot found a garden hoe and it popped up and hit me in the face. Of course they were the ones that wound up laughin' at my sore forehead and me. I guess my haste to say yes to Adren could have been partly because I was the only one left unmarried, and besides, Adren was a good-lookin' man.

We got married the last day of April 1935. He had three pennies in his pocket. Adren had to go the day before to Mount Ida to get our marriage license. It cost three dollars that he borrowed from Dad. We got Justice of the Peace John Golden to come over on a Tuesday. I ain't sure if we paid him anything. For my weddin' outfit, I had just made me a new yellow and pale green striped dress, and that is what I wore. Adren wore his plain overalls and blue-gray shirt. We stood in front of the fireplace that I helped build just a few years before and took our vows. Our honeymoon began that afternoon by layin' by the Irish taters. The next day, we plowed corn. Business just went right along and we all worked in the fields.

Adren's sister Daisy didn't like me for a while. Daisy said, "I was just an old backwoods girl." She wanted him to divorce me. At that point I hadn't even seen a flushin' toilet and didn't know what one was. Adren didn't listen to her, and we toughed it out. Daisy's tune changed to pride years later as my fiddle carried me into the focus of all the folks who saw me perform.

Adren was not ready to settle down, but he stayed right there with Dad and me for a year. My dad was goin' to show Adren how to make knives, fix and sharpen plows, and upset axes in the blacksmith shop — things I already knew how to do. Dad had a small anvil, the bellows, and a small furnace with very little tools. He welded wagon tires and attached them onto the wagons. He made his knife out of a file. He even wanted to show Adren how to work on a fiddle, but Adren didn't take to him and didn't stick with him much. He did later learn to play guitar and could sing pretty good.

My marriage did change some things. I got busier and had little time for playin' or makin' fiddles. If I did pick a fiddle up at night, he said, "Put that d*** thing up and let's go to bed!" So my fiddle mostly hung on the wall for the next twenty-seven years, from 1935 to 1961. In those early days I learned Adren was scared to death of honeybees. The few times he helped he would cover himself with a veil to keep from gettin' stung, so Dad and I would mainly go work the thirty-five hives. With anything good that comes in life, there was always work and sometimes hardship that came along with it. I think workin' the bees reflected that well. To get the sweet out of the hives; you had to endure a few stingers along the way. That first year of our marriage was a new phase in my life. Though day-to-day was not much different, it certainly foretold of the sweet times that were in store — and some of the stingers that would eventually find their way into our home.

Evaline and Lester Peden, and two of their children in 1937.

Violet and Adren
Hensley
with
Wash Brumley
and Beatrice in 1936.

From left are some of Adren Hensley's family members — Arthur; Oscar; George; father, Dave; Daisy; mother, Savannah, holding Adren; Ella Mae; Sally Ann; and Fred.

A new place of our own

Just as my forefathers and foremothers looked for greener grass in their lives, there came a time about a year into my new marriage with Adren that we began our own journey. Maybe it was Adren's itchy feet; maybe it was the relationship he and my Dad had as they tried to work together on the farm. But staying there on the family farm was somethin' that was not in store for us.

Before we started new somewhere else, we had to add one more thing that was brand new to the both of us — a child. We named her Beatrice. The day she was born, February 8, 1936, I took the old iron wash pot my grandmother gave my mother the day she was married, filled it with water, and placed it over a fire. In a washtub, I mixed some of that warm water with cold water, then added more water to the iron pot to boil. I got to scrubbin' the clothes in the washtub, put the worst-soiled ones over in the boilin' water, then took them out of the pot and rinsed them in the rinse tub. I twisted them in my hands to ring them out and hung them on the line. Using the rinse water, I washed the floors with a broom. After a piece, I brought the dry clothes in. Having a baby didn't change things then like it does today. Daily chores came and had to be done.

I wondered how I might know when it was time. I was never around anyone with little ones, and with mama dying when I was so young, I hadn't learned what to expect. I don't remember what time of night it started. I begin to feel a hurt. I knew it was time because I had pains in my lower back. Adren went after the midwife, and she was there before Beatrice was born in the living room. I wasn't in labor long — about four or five hours. I figure it was so short because I was in such good shape. I had muscles like an ox. Before I got pregnant, I could put my right hand behind Adren's knees and my left hand on his chest and flip him over my shoulder. I could wrestle with him and throw him every time — and he was really tryin'. He later got strong after he went in the Army.

The neighbors had given me a little shower and gave me little home-made gowns, a bundle of safety pins, and homemade booties. We bought cloth by the yard made especially for diapers, which we fold corner to corner. The cloth we used was just wide enough to cut off a square and hem it.

Once Beatrice came into the world, it is a wonder I hadn't-a killed her. When she was born, I kept her wrapped good, covering up her head and ears. She slept in the same bed we slept in. A lot of times she would be sweating. I never had any experience around babies, and I later learned you didn't have to keep them covered up, head and ears. I was scared to death she would get cold. She grew right along and started walking at about ten months old. I made her first walking shoes out of that same calfskin we tanned after Mom died and a squirrel skin I had tanned later. The soles were made out of the calfskin, and the uppers were squirrel skin. They were little bitty 'cause she had little bitty feet.

It weren't too long, about three weeks, when Adren came home one day drivin' a borrowed Model T truck and said we were moving to Crystal Springs. This was the first I had heard of it. He didn't tell me he was goin' lookin' for a job. This is probably when I let go of my early thoughts of what our marriage would be. I had no real road map as to how a marriage was supposed to be. I didn't see enough of Mom and Dad together to know theirs. The only reflection I saw were some of my uncles and aunts. They seemed to get on well and have similar likes, and they would do things together and work to make their farms a success.

Adren had told me he wanted to be a farmer, but here he was wantin' to leave our farm. So I gathered our few clothes from the nails behind the doors. There were no closets in the houses back in those days. You could tell my dad was very sad about us goin', but he decided to just load his toolbox and trunk and move with us. Adren wanted to move away from my dad, but it didn't work.

As we drove off to Crystal Springs, I looked out the window of our

Model T and watched years of work grow more and more distant. I knew our marriage would be different than I had pictured. Did I get angry? Not really. I was very disappointed at the time. I would have rather stayed and farmed there, but he was my husband. I was taught that you cleave to your husband. I guess I had to pull together new hopes for what our lives together would be. We weren't through with farmin', but in my mind, I knew that is not what our lives would dance around.

We moved to a tenant house on Homer Bate's farm in Crystal Springs, Arkansas, in March of 1936. Adren worked with Homer side by side on the farm. Adren didn't like to plow and farm for himself, though he didn't mind workin' for someone else. I can't remember Adren gettin' paid cash-wise, but we had a place to live and food to eat off the farm. Dad just stayed at the house with me, and since they did not have to work out in the fields together like on our farm, he and Adren always got along all right. But Adren had an independent streak about him and didn't want my dad in the house with us. Those feet got to itchin' agin on up in December, and we loaded up and moved back to Dad's farm in Alamo. When we were there, Adren accepted things a little more. Maybe workin' down there for Mr. Bates changed his mind a bit about life.

So Daisy "Dell" and Clifford Pate and my sister Dorothy and Jim went to Dyess Colony in Mississippi County, Arkansas, under a farm administration program. This is the community that young Johnny Cash grew up in after his parents resettled there under the same farm program. They got Adren to come down with them, and he wanted me to go, but I stayed with Dad on the home place. We just kept puttin' off goin' down there until it started rainin' in January. It rained until whole houses were going down the Mississippi River. I saw pictures in the paper where just two foot of a high line post were stickin' up out of the water with a chicken sitting on it. It became one of the worst floods in the state's history. At first, the flooding caused them to put their belongings upstairs, and eventually authorities began evacuating the residents. We didn't have phones; I don't know how we got in contact with them.

Dorothy and Jim were sent to Wichita, Kansas. Adren, Dell, and Clifford were sent to Little Rock. A whole bunch of people got sick with typhoid, diphtheria, and other diseases. Adren had to help with the other sick folks, and he became real constipated. They were giving him castor oil, but it wasn't doing him no good. When they gave him a dose, he told them, "Give me that bottle," and he turned it up and drank it. He said, "I got results! I stayed all night in the bathroom after that." When he came home, he swam the Mizarn Creek with it up and muddy with his clothes on, but he made it. I guess in a way the flood saved me from another move for a couple more years.

Dad would say "Kids, its time to go to work." More or less we all worked along together. I think though I took the lead as much as my dad did. When we settled back in at Alamo, Adren would do whatever jobs he could get; he worked for Levi and Ola Powell for 50 cents a day mending fences, helping make a crop, and cutting timber. There weren't many folks that could hire things done. We didn't have much money or a lot a food, but we never starved to death.

Come spring of the year, I would pick all the wild plants that could be eaten. We would snatch up poke greens, chicken pepper, dandelions, plantain, wild lettuce, sour dock, fennel, and lamb's quarter. I didn't know at the time we could eat pursalene, but I learned later on. Lamb's quarter was more plentiful. I learned later that the Indians in that area, Quapaw, used to cultivate it. We would put it in the pot with the poke greens and boil it down and squeeze the water out. Put it in a skillet with bacon grease, and fry it a little while, break an egg in it and fry it, and you get good poke greens. It's not a laxative then.

We didn't have a cow, and we didn't buy fresh milk. We'd either buy a can of Pet Milk or Milnot Milk. I breastfed all the kids. The last three or four, I started out breastfeeding, but I was like the old cow that dried up. I put them on Milnot Milk mixed with a certain amount of water. I started them on table food just as soon as they could take blended food. Take a fork and mash taters or pinto beans up, so they soon learned to eat.

We didn't stuff our stomachs; occasionally we would have a good meal if we had a good supply of fresh cabbage out of the garden or fresh berries out of the woods. Normally it was enough to keep us going. I was always strong as a mule. I always wanted to use my full strength. After a hard day, Adren would come in tired and ask me to pull off his shoes and say "Aw, honey will you wash my feet?" I did for a long time until one day I realized, my feet was in the same shape. Somewhere one day about 1938, I told him I was so tired from daily work. "Pull your own shoes off. I am too tired," I said. Gradually, he got out of the habit of asking. I still pulled his socks off and ran them between his toes for years after that. You don't have time to get bored with life on the farm, and before I knew it I was having our second child — Marvin — on Feb. 21, 1938. The labor was a little shorter this time. When he was two months old, Dr. Stewart said he had double pneumonia and gave me some kind of medicine and he got over it pretty quick. When he was four months old, I would put Marvin on a baby quilt under the apple tree in our garden while I worked the garden. When it came time to go to the house, I picked up the baby and told Beatrice to get the baby's quilt. There must have been ants under the quilt, and when Sister (as we called her) picked up the quilt, she said, "I'll just be shang-damned at the ants!" I don't know where she got that. I never cursed, but Dad said a few curse words.

Further along in that year, Wallace Cannon's cows kept comin' up near our house. Animals weren't fenced in then. The crops were protected with split rail fences or picket fences. Dad chased them out of the yard and remarked that he ought to get his shotgun and shoot them sons-a-bitchin' cows. Sister was standing in the kitchen door and saw the cows coming back and said, "Oh, Gwoupa! Get your shootgun and shoot them sons-a-bitchin' tows!"

We farmed there two more seasons in Alamo. During this year Adren also picked up some work through a WPA* project across the mountain helping build a bridge over Collier's Creek. We use to have to just ford or wade it. This bridge allowed us to cross when the water was up.

After I got married, I cried more the first several years than I did when I was growin' up. One day I was sittin' there cryin' over somethin' that Adren had done or said — I can't remember what it was. Sister, was about two, looked up at me and said, "Mommy, don't cry." I remember thinkin', "She is so sweet, I hate to see her grow up." I know when he said somethin' that hurt my feelin's, instead of fussin' back with him I would go off somewhere and cry. If you made your bed hard, you slept on it. I was married, and you made a vow for better or worse.

He didn't seem to have a way with the babies. He didn't want to hold them. He'd take the baby a while and they would cry. A few times he would say, 'You take the baby and let me stir the cookin'.' I have held the baby in one arm and stirred the cookin' or used the washboard washing clothes with the other. As they got older, he would play the games with them and carry them around on his shoulder.

Sometimes as I think back, I should have bought me a bunch of foot powder; maybe it would have relaxed Adren's itchin' feet and kept us in one place for longer. Once again, December was here and we were gonna be moving. We had a little more warning on this one, so, when we started to go to Oden, Dad made a deal with my brother-in-law, Jim, and my

* The Works Progress Administration, or WPA, was started under President Roosevelt as part of the New Deal. It was renamed the Work Projects Administration in 1939.

sister, Dorothy Pate, to move in with him on the farm. They continued farming there when we left. We lived at Oden in the direction of the Ouachita Mountains. We joined a farm home administration loan program at Mount Ida. They let you buy a team of horses and make a crop and then pay the money back. We got a good team of little horses and moved up there in a wagon just before Christmas in 1939. We put what we had in the wagon. We didn't have too many clothes, just a few pieces for each child and somethin' for Adren and me. We had a bedstead and a mattress, a few cooking vessels — skillet, pots to cook beans in — shovel and hoes, choppin' ax, and a shepherd dog named Tubby. He was a good squirrel dog and good to drive the cows.

The place had an old house; part of it was logs, with one big rundown room that had a passel of cracks in it. We shut off that part of the house so we wouldn't lose the heat. The kitchen and living room were the log section, and it had a bedroom and a porch built on. It had a little barn there, and we had a cow along for milk. The barn and house could use repair, and the fences had gone down.

We started breaking soil plantin' taters and English peas in March. I liked to plow with the horses. We had a sorrel named Dolly and a dark brown one with a dot in its forehead that we called Dot. Dot really worked good with a plow. We had to put up sticks and wire up tall as me for the peas to run up on. I canned twenty-five quarts that season. Only year I canned that many English peas. They really growed good. We also planted corn, but our money crop was cotton.

We had a claw hammer with a handle broken off to only about six inches long. We would buy my oldest son Marvin nails and give him a board, and he would drive them in. Adren was bad to sit with his legs stretched out with his feet crossed. He would come in and tell the kids to "Run along now. Daddy's tired. Scram!" to get them out of his way. Marvin came by his dad with the hammer, hollered "Cram Daddy!" and threw that hammer right at his feet. If Adren hadn't moved his feet, he would have been hit.

One time, Marvin came out of the bedroom off to the side of the kitchen, and for some reason a little toy I had made him gave him a start. I had made him a little stuffed dog out of a piece of old wore out black coat. The little dog was lying just inside the door of the bedroom, and when he came out of there, it caught his eye and it scared him so bad. We had to console him for quite a long time after that. He eventually realized the creature from the dark was his loyal companion.

Calvin was born there at the house in Oden on January 16, 1940. I never went to a doctor for none of my pregnancies, not one time. Adren insisted on this one we have a doctor for the birth. By now, my labors weren't goin' much more than thirty minutes or so. When labor started, Adren rode the horse to the neighbor's and asked them to call the doctor. He returned, and Calvin was already comin', so Adren had to do the doctor's part. The doctor arrived about two hours later. He looked at everything and said, "I couldn't done a better job myself." We still had to pay him the twenty dollars. The midwife would have only cost five. That was the last time we had a doctor, except when Sandy was born.

A few weeks later, I went out to milk the cow and came back to find my four-year-old daughter had this brand new baby, about three weeks old, laying across the chair changing his diaper. It scared me a little bit, but she cared for him real good. I told Sister, "Oh, Sister, be careful with the baby. I am glad you didn't hurt him."

Adren sort of got tired of the grind of the farm, or maybe his feet got itchy again. On a trip to visit his sister Daisy, and Clifford, they talked him into leaving the farm in Oden and moving to Hemp Wallace, which is now part of Hot Springs. So, Adren let everything we had worked on there fall through. The horses went back, and this time we moved in September with a borrowed truck. I looked out the windows of that truck at the fields we planted. Corn and cotton were growin', comin' into themselves, and I hoped someone would get the benefit of the work we had done.

We moved in with his brother and sister-in-law, George and Leona Hensley. They were rentin' a house from John Hellam with three bedrooms, a livin' room, and a kitchen. We used one of the bedrooms as our kitchen and shared the livin' room. They had a bedroom, and we had a bedroom. Calvin and George's boy, Junior, were babies about three months apart. Dell and Clifford came to visit and asked their boy, Raymond, which baby he thought was cuter, and Raymond said, "Calvin, cause he grins like a possum!"

In Hemp Wallace, Adren went to work in John's sawmill there for a while, before he got a job cuttin' stave bolts. Stave bolts are cut into strips called staves. The wooden slats were used to make barrels and they were cut from white oak. Our next home was a tent in the woods near a creek nestled among the white oaks that Adren and the other workers cut to send to the mill. It was late November or early December 1941; of course we couldn't take a lot with us, so we had to leave some things back at his brother's house including my late mother's dresses. Could you imagine, livin' in a tent outside in the winter day after day? Well it weren't as bad as it might sound. It was rather comfortable. The old gray tent was pretty good size. It was long enough we had two beds in it lengthways and one turned crossways. We had a cook stove and a little pot bellied heater stove. The tent had a pole right in middle of it lengthways, and we would drive nails there to hang clothes. We put dirt up around the edges of the bottom end of the tent so the cold would not come in. I sewed two tow sacks together lengthways and then two more and then sewed them end-ways together, which made two sacks wide, and four long. That was the walkway in the door on the dirt floor of the tent. When they got full of dirt, I would take them sacks and shake the dirt out. That was how I swept the floor. We brought a few clothes, which we hung on nails; our skillets and pots; and some canned stuff; along with us to our new home. We mainly cooked pinto beans and taters. We would cook oatmeal and rice for breakfast. Sometimes I made biscuits and gravy. We didn't have a kitchen cabinet. We just had an open box with a door to set the cooking vessels in.

Another one of Adren's brothers — Fred — moved in with us for about a month there in the tent and worked with him. He weighed about 200 pounds, and he would come in and his overalls would be soakin' wet with sweat. I would wash them out in the creek and hang them out on a bent-over bush. After Fred left, we had another man that worked there — Al Bean — and his son Franklin that stayed with us two or three months working with Adren.

It came a snow about four or five inches deep while we were there after Christmas. We had baked a cake for Christmas; that was all we could do. We didn't have any money to buy toys or anythin' for the children. While working at the mill, Adren had bought an old black Model T. His nephew Raymond Jones was visiting us when the snow came in and Adren had to crank that car. It wouldn't start, and he got so mad that he threw that crank and it went down way under the snow. His nephew was under the wheel trying to start it; we had to hide our faces to keep Adren from seein' us laughin'. We had to wait until the snow melted to find it. Adren had us bring coals of fire out there to warm the engine and start it without the crank.

Calvin turned two years old there. I remember one time Adren was givin' him a whippin' for some mischief. Calvin stopped cryin' all of a sudden, looked up at him, and said "Ow, Daddy, that hurts!" The comment amused Adren so much that stopped the whippin'.

Greener pastures called to us in the spring and so we went next to Arkadelphia. Adren got a job workin' on a farm for Morris "Mutt" Daniel and his wife Edie. He grew corn and raised hay for the animals. They also raised chickens. We lived in the Daniels' tenant house on the edge of the highway with the farm back behind the houses. I sewed and helped mend clothes for Morris and his wife. One day, our little dog, Tiny, ran into the street. Calvin went after it, and a semi truck liketa got Calvin, stopping with a screech of its brakes. Calvin saved the dog out of the road. Marvin was four years old, and Morris's boy was three but bigger than Marvin. So Marvin got his hand-me-downs. I remember one time the little boy was sittin' on a nail keg — a small barrel made to hold nails — at their house, abusin' it, and Mutt called him down. Someone else visitin' said to Mutt, "What's the big deal? It's only a nail keg." Mutt said, "Someday, we may have nice furniture. He needs to learn to take care of a nail keg so he'll take care of the furniture." When we were at Arkadelphia, Adren bought this roadster; it was red and had a rumble seat. Payments were five dollars a month. We had that when we moved from Arkadelphia to Pearcy in September. We didn't stay for the fall harvest. We visited with his sister Dell, and she talked Adren into comin' up to Pearcy. Adren went back to Arkadelphia and got our little belongings — bedstead and mattress, cookstove, a few pots and pans, and a few clothes.

At Pearcy, Adren went to work in a sawmill where he moved the logs around. We lived in a sawmill shack on Highway 70. It was made out of slabs and set in a pine grove. It had a kitchen, two bedrooms, and a livin' room. There was a well and an outhouse. Dell and Clifford and their son, Raymond, who was about seventeen, lived nearby. One day, Raymond talked Adren into lettin' him drive Adren's car to a neighbor's down the road. He took Marvin and Calvin with him. When he was ready to come back, in turnin' the car around, he bumped the back of it into a tree. It did not hurt the car, but he gave Marvin and Calvin a dime each to not say anythin' about it. As soon as he got close enough for us to hear, Calvin, who was a little over two-and-a-half years old, yelled out, "Raymond hit a tree with the car and gave me and Marvin a dime not to tell you, and I lost mine!" He didn't realize he was tellin' on Raymond. He was just tellin' about losin' his dime.

Dell and Clifford stopped by on October 9, 1942, as they were moving to Oklahoma. I bathed the kids and put them to bed. Dell and Clifford marveled at Calvin walkin' to bed in his sleep. They left about 11 p.m., not knowin' Russell would arrive about an hour later. Four months later we were on the road again, this time because of the lure of a job in the Bauxite mines near Hot Springs. Bauxite was used to make aluminum. We settled on Vista Heights Street, or Tin Can Hill, up from the railroad track in Hot Springs.

There were lots of little kids in the neighborhood. One particular six-year-old boy had a reputation for meanness. He came to our house, and Sister, who was also six years old, was standin' with her back to the couch. He drew his fist back and said, "I'm gonna bloody your nose!" Sister beat him to the draw and popped him in the nose first. He went home then but kept coming back. When he came back he started to mistreat our kids' few toys so I said, "You wouldn't want them to go to your house and treat your toys like that, would you?" or if he was bullying someone, I'd say, "You wouldn't want him to treat you that way, would you?" If the kids had to stack wood, I'd say, "Come help us stack wood." We included him in all we did around the house. By the time we left, the neighbors didn't mind him comin' over anymore. His grandparents said I did more for him in six months than his parents had done in six years. In Hot Springs is where I tried to ride roller skates for the first and only time. Some kid from across the street left them at our house after he forgot to take them home with him. I put on the skates and rolled right under the table, turnin' the table upside down right on top of me! I took them off and said, "I ain't tryin' that no more!" I did try ice skating, though, many years later. I didn't have any luck with that either.

Adren had worn out another car by the time we were in Hot Springs, so he had to get up early to go to work by bicycle. I would try to wake him up at three o'clock in morning. At the mine, he oiled and greased the heavy equipment there and was an all-around mechanic.

We received word from Adren's oldest sister, Sally Ann, that her husband, Admerle York, got real bad sick. So we headed off to Vandervoort, Arkansas. One of his other brothers, Ott Hensley, was visitin' from Ringgold, Oklahoma, at the same time. Admerle passed away while we were there.

Ott told Adren he would trade him forty acres at Sobol, Oklahoma, for the two-seated square-backed Ford sedan we were driving. By this time, Adren had saved up enough to buy it second-handed. Before I could say "shoo fly," Adren made the trade and we were off again to start over somewhere else. Adren borrowed Ott's pickup, came back to Vista

Heights and got our bedding, cook stove, and heater stove and all the rest; but to my frustration, he left my box of recipes, and off we headed to Oklahoma. As I look back on all the moves, I really didn't want to move that much. Each time it meant sayin' goodbye to neighbors and making new friends where we went. The kids always seem to be excited when we went to a new place; they never did complain about changing schools once they were in school.

Oklahoma was the next land of milk and honey for us. Well, I knew there would be a cow in it somewhere from which I would be pullin' our milk. As far as the honey, there would be some of that too — mixed in among the "stingers" I had grown to know so well from the time I was tending my dad's bees.

Adren and Violet Hensley hug in Hot
Springs in 1943.

Adren's sister Daisy "Dell" Pate
and niece Ruby

Adren and Violet Hensley stop in Antlers, Oklahoma in 1946.

Adren's sister Daisy "Dell" Pate and brothers Fred and Ott

Violet, Bonnie Skelton, and Dorothy Vandever in 1945

Calvin Hensley in 1946

Violet Hensley and Senia Seymour in 1945

An Okie from Alamo

I hoped that with this move we would find those greener pastures that would help us sink in some roots. Sobol, Oklahoma, is in the southeastern part of the state in Pushmataha County. We arrived in December 1943 at its crossroads to find the community had a little grocery store and a gas station. Up the road a bit was the community school. That was about the size of it.

We paused just long enough there to stretch our legs before headin' out to our new home on that 40-acre farm bought with a car. For Adren, that wasn't much of a sacrifice. Cars didn't last him long. He would tear up the transmission or throw a rod in the engine. When we rolled onto the farm, it was easy to see it had not seen a broom nor plow in years. We had already been in such open, leaky old houses that this one didn't seem much different. The house was a dogtrot cabin — two rooms, with a front and back entry directly across from each other in each room and a four- or five-foot space between the two rooms called the dogtrot that was open to the outdoors except for the roof. It kept the heat from the kitchen out of the livin' quarters in the summertime. Each room also had side doors in the front corners of the rooms so you could walk from one room across the dogtrot and stay under the roof out of the rain to get to the other room. The dogtrot space had been boarded up at each end with sawmill slabs nailed up and down. The livin' room was on the south end with the front entry to the west.

Upon entry, there was just room to fit two full-size beds — one for Adren and me, and one for the four kids. Later, we sat a car seat on the south end of the room opposite the foot of the beds. That was our couch. The kitchen had room for the dinner table and the wood cook stove with nails in the wall to hang my pots and pans on. Later, Dad would spend a few months with us, and he would sleep on a cot in the dogtrot room. It had a little smokehouse at the west end of the house that eventually, come summer, would be covered with the most beautiful pink roses.

Of course, I couldn't tell what was in store for us when I first saw our new home. Old and abandoned, it was still our home, and I had to make it where we could have a place to sleep and eat that night. We had to begin by gettin' some wood in and buildin' a fire in the heater stove and cuttin' wood for the cook stove. We had to locate our water, which we brought from a spring in front of the house. We had a few wooden boxes and a bench to gather up around the table for chairs. So we made our evenin' meal and then set up our beds and prepared for a night of rest before the real work began.

We didn't let no grass grow under our feet. Startin' the next day we prepared for winter by gatherin' wood to last a while, and then we started mendin' the fences and cleanin' the ground to make a garden. We didn't grow any corn that first year. The next year we had a little crop of corn between the house and barn. Mostly, Adren worked over at nick-knack jobs for somebody else — mendin' a fence, helpin' at a sawmill, or workin' on a car. Those jobs didn't bring much money.

While I thought World War II had passed our little family by, the arrival of a letter as we had spring plantin' changed that, and Adren had to go into the service. Adren had tried to volunteer back in 1942, but they would not take him since he had young children. Despite his having even more children, this time they took him anyway. R.G. was born on April 2, 1944. When Adren reported to the U.S. Army, they found out he had a new son and gave him some extra time at home before sendin' him to basic trainin'.

On a visit to our neighbor, Adren got the measles, so the Army gave him another thirty days, but eventually he did have to report and go through trainin' before bein' shipped out to the Pacific. He went for boot camp in May, and we stayed in contact by letters. When he shipped out overseas though, I didn't hear from him for forty-nine days. When I finally did, we had a bundle of letters from him. He told me he got a bundle from me about the same time. From the Army, I was gettin' a little check of $100 a month. Usin' it, I had our place fenced in and bought a new wagon, a team of mules, and hay to feed them on. I was able to get a couple of milk cows. We had a few chickens, which provided eggs that I would sell off once in a while. There was a grocery store nearby where I could get flour and salt, bakin' powder and soda. By then, we had to buy meal sometimes. Food was a lot cheaper then; I cooked beans and taters for dinner and taters and beans for supper with cornbread or milk.

We had to buy feed in one hundred-pound sacks, and I saved the feed sacks and made the boys shirts and the girls and me dresses out of them. The sacks were flower prints, checks, stripes, or just plain white. I even sewed four feed sacks together for a sheet for the bed. I wore them sheets out boilin' them in the washpot and scrubbin' them on the scrub board. I pieced quilts out of every scrap I could get. We bought flour in twenty-five-pound sacks that were white. I made diapers, dish towels, and Sister's slips out of those. Neighbors would come around, and I cut hair or did sewin' for them free. I made clothes by hand with needle and thread. I always wished I could do for other people; I didn't realize until someone else told me years later that I was doin' for other people all along. We made a vegetable garden and grew flowers — zinnias and marigolds. I often shared the extras from the garden with our neighbors who didn't have what we grew, and they did the same with us.

It was almost ten months before Adren reached the front lines in March of 1945 in Luzon in the Philippines. The Allies were workin' to take control of Luzon. He told me later that he told his captain that he had a feelin' if he went out that mornin', he was goin' to get hit. He was out on the line four days when he was hit on March 24, 1945. I found out somethin' was wrong when I got a letter from him that didn't read right. It said somethin' about him bein' OK. Then I got a card from the government sayin' that he was wounded and was in a specific hospital. I remember bein' thankful that he was alive. After he was injured, he had someone else write me a letter. I could tell it wasn't his handwritin'. Back then, because of the wartime restrictions, he wasn't allowed to tell anything that happened. Then I got another card when the Army shipped him back to the states.

Adren was sent to Temple, Texas, for a while in June and by August to McAllister, Oklahoma. I went by bus a couple of times to McAllister and saw him. It was more or less a convalescent place. I tried to talk with him about the experience he had been through. He wasn't able to write about it in letters. The Army would have censored it anyway. He didn't say too much about it for a while. Eventually, he told me how the bullet came in from the left and hit him right in the chest. He said he had a package of cigarettes and ink pen in his shirt pocket that were hit. The shot came in the center of his chest and came out under his arm and through his right elbow. When he came to himself, they told him he had been dead momentarily. They bolted his right arm together. It was much smaller than the other as a result. They let him come home for a couple of thirty-day furloughs beginnin' in July. That's when he worked on buildin' the barn. He built the biggest part of the barn with his left arm though he didn't get it completed before havin' to return to the convalescent place. I went to visit him by bus in August and September. I had to leave the children at home. My oldest daughter, Sister, by then was twelve, and she and the neighbors looked after the younger ones.

Soon, it became apparent Adren's right arm would never be the same. A year passed before he could reach his mouth with that limb. He only got ninety percent disability total and temporary from his wound, and he received a little check. The Army didn't release him until November 1945.

After he got out of service, he came home and immediately began makin' some changes to what I had been doin' in his absence. I realized early in my marriage with Adren that he was partial to drink. He had worked with moonshiners before we were married, and he grew a taste for the liquor. The first time it really was noticeable was one night when I had some of my neighbor Darlene Wheeler's family over. Adren came in, and before we knew it he had her young baby holdin' it up in one hand. Everyone was scared he was goin' to drop the baby and we all were holdin' our breath. He finally handed it back to Darlene, and we all breathed again. In those early years, drinkin' wasn't that much of a problem. We didn't have any money, so there really wasn't any to spend on it. Holidays like the Fourth of July, Thanksgiving, or Christmas, were a sure reason for him to go out with some of his drinkin' friends and come in three sheets to the wind. He'd come in, sleep it off, and the next mornin' he'd be okay. As I look back on my marriage, it is safe to say this is one part of it I wish I could erase.

The war left deep physical and mental scars, and Adren's drinkin' only worsened as time passed. After his return home to Oklahoma, Adren's desire to expand his drinkin' beyond holidays increased. It wasn't unusual for him to go on a bender that would last for days. He'd go off and come home the next day, usually at night, sometimes in the early hours of the mornin', after drinkin' with his friends. I was always uneasy when he was off like that, and I would lay awake listenin' for him to drive up to the house. I remember one night when I heard him comin', the truck was makin' such a racket. It sounded like he had the gas floored with one foot while holdin' down the brake with the other. When I heard him comin' I'd get all shaky inside. One time about eleven o'clock, I remember tremblin' so much I made the bed shake. Now I didn't shake because I was scared of him. I was more afraid for him than me. It was nerve rackin'. I didn't like to see anybody drunk. People just are not themselves when they are. Adren was not himself when he came in that way. Adren never hurt me when he was drunk, he'd just come in wobblin' around and want me to cook him a meal.

Sometimes he might say somethin' that he might not say without the drink, but I would never get in word fights with him. I was always disappointed, but I didn't argue with him. He always said of me, "If I ride up to the door and throw my hat in and she threw it back out, I would know I was not welcome." One day just for fun, he rode his horse Rex up and tossed his hat in, and I just tossed it back. He went off two or three days before he came back. I just done it for fun. This is when he might come back with somethin' like, "It's what you don't say is what makes me mad," tryin' to get me to word fight with him. When he sobered up, he often said, "I'm sorry, I've got to quit drinkin'." But it was hard for him to resist next time it was handy.

Besides taking time away from the family, the biggest problem that drink brought into our home was the waste of money. Before the war, we didn't have much cash, and durin' the war, I was able to build up what the family had on the $100 the Army sent us each month. I controlled the money, saw our needs were met, and kept addin' to what we had. When Adren returned, that $100 became $110 for his service disability. Even though I still handled the money from his check, Adren saw this as his money. Any money he worked out he didn't bring it to me; he saw that as his exclusively. Unlike me, he didn't see makin' sure the family needs were met first as important. If he thought he needed a car and had the money, he bought it. If it needed a tire or a part, he got it. And if he wanted to go on a bender and buy moonshine, he did it. If he didn't have what he needed, then he asked me for money from the check.

We had a bootlegger in the area one time that he owed sixteen dollars. When his check came in, I thought he should pay the grocery man, but that wasn't his thinkin'. He went and paid the moonshiner. He said that the grocery man can sue you and take your cow for his bill, but the moonshiner can't 'cause his business is supposed to be hidden. His approach to life in this way just meant I had to work harder to provide food from the land and the woods to feed us. While I was able to take $100 a month and with five children meet our needs and build things up, because of his drinkin' and his need to support an automobile, he took us in the other direction where we owed money while receivin' $110 per month. I wasn't happy about this, but it was what it was. We married for better or worse, and this was part of the latter. We just made do with what we had.

Adren used to say, "You'd squeeze a penny 'til it squealed." I'd tell him, "I'm just economical." He couldn't find a job right away after returnin', so he began sellin' the cows off. By that time I had two milk cows and three heifers I had bought. We managed to stretch them along for about three years. I remember we had gotten groceries on credit, and we paid the bill to the grocer with our last cow. The grocer was nice, though, and let us keep the cow for almost a year in 1948 to have milk for our youngest — Eddie, who was born July 3. After we ran out of cows, Adren got some odd jobs and worked off and on that year cuttin' billets, which helped with the bills.

We decided to build another house in 1948 right up next to the spring. The spring branch ran right through the property from the west to the east of the house. Down along that branch there was a swamp of sweetgum trees — a sweetgum thicket. We never did cultivate it. At that time there was some kind of poison. We took an ax and chopped a circle around the tree and put the liquid poison in there, and the trees all died. The next year or two they all fell. It made a little bit more grass for the cow and the horse.

Adren was able to buy the lumber from some run down buildin's to build the house. We moved in June, even before the floorin' was done, especially in our bedroom. So we slept in the livin' room, and that is where Eddie was born. The house had five rooms — three bedrooms, a livin' room, and kitchen. It had a small back porch. In the spring of '53, we got our first electricity in a house. One bedroom came off the livin' room, and the other two off the kitchen. We could also pass through between all three bedrooms. We still did not have runnin' water, and we would only have electricity a few months.

When we would make homemade ice cream in the new house, my horse Tony had a second sense about it, and he would make his way to

the window of the house lookin' to get a servin' of his own. He like doin'
the same to get a cookie from the kids. One time, Sister gave him one
standin' in the door, and he was lookin' for another from her, and she
blew in his face. He didn't like that. I thought he was goin' to come in the
house after her, so I shut the door. He must have heard her runnin'
through the house towards the back door because there he was waitin' on
her. He couldn't get in that door though because of the little porch.

I bought Tony in 1945 from Archie Hawthorne. I paid fifty dollars for
the horse and had to wait and save up some money to buy the saddle for
forty dollars. When I got him, Tony was five years old, very gentle, but
spoiled rotten. His mother had died, so they raised him on cow's milk.
When I milked the cow, I had to hide the bucket in the corn crib until I
was ready to go to the house or he'd drink the milk. He drunk the whole
bucket once. I broke him to ride. After I had him trained good, I could
grab the saddle horn and swing into the saddle. Usually I used the stirrup,
however, and when my foot touched the stirrup, he was already movin'. If
there were other horses and riders, he would be runnin'. He never wanted
to be left behind. Adren said Tony knew I liked it, and that's why he did
it. Although he was always anxious to get started, if I had a baby in my
arms he was a different horse. He would stand still for me to mount and
move along real easy. He seemed to know when I really needed him to be
gentle.

I once took my three- or four-week-old baby with me to the neighbor's house for a clutch of settin' eggs. I managed to get them back without crackin' an egg — even though I had to dismount and remount with
the baby and the eggs in order to open and close the gate. Sister, age
twelve; Marvin, ten; and Calvin, eight; would ride Tony to school until
Russell was old enough to go to school as well. Durin' one such event in
winter after school was dismissed, it was rainin', freezin' as it fell, and
everything and everyone was dressed in icicles by the time they reached
home. I was offered a one-year-old car for Tony, but I wouldn't have sold
him for any amount of money. I taught him to give me a kiss, hug my
neck, rear up on command, and to paw the ground when I asked him if he
was hungry. I could pull the reins over his neck and lift up a little on his
front foot, and he would lay down. I shod that horse for twenty-two years.

Tony could turn on a dime and give you back the change. I rode him
many miles. One day I rode him from Sobol to Hugo, came back by
Antlers, and then back to Sobol — about sixty-five miles. I ran him a lot.
At Caddo Gap, Arkansas, the train track ran alongside the road, and I

raced with the train. When I slacked up, the guy in the engine hollered, "Come on! Come on!" I yelled back "You can only run a horse so far before you kill him!" People told me I would kill him before he was ten years old. He was a toughie or I guess I would've. He lived to be twenty-seven years, four months, and two days old. Eventually, Adren bought himself a saddle horse too, a big, long-legged black named Rex that could really step out and run. I loved handlin' horses and mules and could get them to do things for me that were amazin' simply because they knew how much I cared. My knowledge about them and the way I had with them came from watchin' my dad work with ours when I was a little girl.

After bein' away from my dad for so long, it was a great joy to have him come spend the summer of 1946 with us. He added so much to the day-to-day activities of the children. Up to this point, the kids really did not know their grandfather because they were too young when he was around them. He would sit in the yard and play his fiddle for them. He provided a good audience for the kid's adventures as they created make believe around the old hickory tree. Often when they felt a little mischievous, and I wasn't in sight, Marvin and Calvin would climb the hickory and send a nut sailin' down towards his hat restin' below in the shade. Anticipatin' what was comin' though, Dad kept one step ahead of them, movin' slightly, and seemin' unphased, except on occasion when he would step out from the bench under the tree to see who was bombin' him. Then he would proceed to give that child a piece of his mind. He left us to go back to Alamo with Dorothy after that summer, to our home place.

When we said our goodbyes, it was our last time to stand in front of one another and embrace. He became bedfast in 1947, I think possibly with leukemia. He was paralyzed and couldn't move. A letter from Dorothy told me of his situation. I knew not bein' able to play the fiddle anymore brought sadness to him. I managed to scrape up the money to get a bus ticket to Alamo, Arkansas, in January 1948 to see Dad and discovered what they had shared with me in the letter. He couldn't talk much anymore. I don't recall us talkin' at all. I just sat in a chair by his bed for a couple of days and tried to be a comfort to him. At the end of my visit, I leaned over and wrapped my arms around his shoulders, and said. "I got to go back home now, Dad." We didn't say, "I love you" in those days. It was by actions and in our looks to one another that conveyed that. As I left the room, I had to hide my tears from him as I looked back one last time from the door before catchin' my ride to meet the bus. This would be the last time I would see Dad. In fact, I would learn of his passin' later that year in a letter, two weeks after he died June 17, 1948. He was already buried when I got the letter the day before my son Eddie was born on July 3. Back in those days, they waited to let me know, afraid the news might cause a complication in my pregnancy. They sent some flowers along with the letter from his funeral. I was very sad, but there was a new member of the family comin' into the world, and whether I wanted to give my attention to that or not, he was very insistent that it was his time to appear.

My day-to-day life in Oklahoma brought different tasks each day, but I knew with the first rays of sun peakin' through the window, I'd be up washin' my hands and face and be at the cook stove, fixin' a pot of oatmeal, bakin' biscuits, and makin' gravy. Dependin' on the year I had up to nine children to roust out of bed, help get dressed and motivated towards the table, and do their chores before they were off to school. The kids walked to school about two miles, and each mornin' I made sure their face and hands were washed and hair combed, and in the airish months that their coats were on before they got on their way. Will and Lois Langley's kids - Verna, Hack, and Vera, would be comin' by our place by the time our kids were startin' on their trip to school. Sometimes, dependin' on their ages or if school was out, the children's day's included a steady amount of play because I knew that helped to make children happy, growin', and full of life. After I got the older children off to their chores, school, or play, I would make up the beds, sweep the floors, and gather what was needed for our noon meal. Those tasks might be bringin' in fresh squash, okra, or tomatoes from the garden, or pullin' out the dry beans and pickin' the bad ones out to get them ready to cook. I'd fry taters and put the dry beans on by ten at night. The oldest kids, such as Sister and Marvin, would get in wood for the cook stove and carry water from the spring and help around the kitchen. The youngest were always close at hand whether sittin' on my hip, lyin' in a bushel basket on pillows, or sittin' on pillows in a chair secured in place with a piece of cloth five or six inches wide. When things for dinner were underway, I might have a pair of pants needin' patchin', or I would continue projects such as piecin' quilts. In the gardenin' months, some of my day would be taken up there, and ultimately some days would be spent washin' clothes. I often stood with a baby on my left hip while scrubbin' clothes on the washboard with my right hand.

The longest days were durin' plantin' and harvest, and that meant we all had to work together. If we were harvestin' beans, that meant pickin', stringin', and snappin', and I would be puttin' them all in the jars and runnin' the pressure cooker from can to can't. If it were corn, the ears had to be pulled. Sister, Marvin, and Calvin would gather them and bring them to the house. The family shucked. I removed the silks then cut the corn from the cob and canned it. These were long days, sometimes wearin' on through the night, and even Adren joined in runnin' the pressure cooker. You couldn't wait, otherwise the vegetables would not be good as they should be in the jars. I had a huge cannin' season in 1948. On average I would can 800 to 1,000 quarts of food every summer, but this year I had over 330 quarts of corn, bringin' the total for the summer to 1,500 quarts.

On the average day though, work continued throughout the afternoon as I looked forward to the children comin' in from school. No matter what I was doin', I always made time for any of the kids that came to me and asked me somethin' or that needed help or wanted to know how to do somethin'. Encouragin' them to take on work projects and odd jobs also helped them learn a great deal. Sister sold seeds from a company for two years. The last year, she got a Dick Tracy camera, which she still has. Calvin sold garden seeds one year and bought a mandolin from Montgomery Ward. At the time, nobody had told me that it was just like the fiddle. He didn't learn to play then, so he left it at my house, and I made a new top and back on it eventually after it came apart. I can pick out tunes on it now, and so can he.

I would prepare for the evenin' meal, and each of the kids would arrive and get after their chores and their homework, and we would all eat together. Of course, once Adren returned from the war, he was there doin' his part, workin' on odd jobs and around the place. In the times when there was a little more daylight or the moon was bright we would get outside and Adren and me would play games or ball or have races with the kids. Other times, he just sat on the porch listenin' to the sounds of the night bugs and frogs, or looked up and picked out shapes from the stars as they started their first twinklin'. We generally hit the bed about the time the sun lowered its shade and night seeped easily through the windows of the house. The evenin' meant all the kids needed a good washin' at the washbowl before their sleepy heads hit the pillows.

With the boys in one bed and girls in another in different rooms, they would sometimes still be full of play, but neither of us allowed our children to rule the roost in any way as many parents do today. If they didn't do right, I would have them disciplined with my hand, a switch, or the razor strap my dad used on me as a girl. He only whipped me three times — once when I broke a fiddle top, once when I got a match out of his trunk, and once when I went to stay overnight with a girlfriend without askin'. My kids didn't have to be told more than once't, and they would do what they were supposed to. I taught them to share and not fuss and fight, to respect others and not to go in the other feller's house and pick up this and that and the other. My kids weren't much trouble except when they got to fussin', and I stopped that right away. Occasionally, one would be in mischief of some kind, and I would come in and ask who did it. None would own up to it, so I would just say, "I'll just punish everyone of you, and then I will get the right one." Before you knew it, the one at fault would come forward. I kept all my kids close. They were home at night, not like so many today, and they were not out prowlin' around town with other kids or goin' out on dates until they left to get out on their own. They never seemed to want to.

Sometimes after the kids were in bed, Adren and me would sit by the fire and I would read to him. The hours would just melt away on us, as I would reach into the novels of Zane Grey, one of his favorite authors. Sometimes at his encouragement, we would find ourselves missin' needed sleep, but this was a special time that we shared throughout our marriage. He loved listenin' to my voice and hearin' me read these adventures that drew us closer, and in a way that was our way of goin' on trips together through the eyes of these authors. There was always somethin' excitin' happening in the books.

Not that there was any lack of excitement in our own lives. One time in 1949, when we had this old car that didn't have no cab on it, Adren took Calvin and Marvin to school. The car had just a flat bed with a board across it for a seat, and a board sticking up for the back of the seat, and a windshield. On such rides, Calvin and Marvin would shut their eyes and try to guess where a rocky spot was in the road. One day, Calvin said, "We are just about to the rough spot." Just about that time, they hit it, and Calvin bounced off. Adren ran over his head. The car had no brakes, so Adren had to put it in reverse and back it up to rush to help him. Instead of taking him on to school, he took him to the doctor. Calvin's left eye had been damaged to the point it reduced his ability to see, and he had some broken ribs. I don't know how it kept from killin' him. No matter how big the kids got, they were still my babies, and I worried and suffered through their aches and pains with them.

At times it seemed I was just gettin' one child out of diapers before another little one was comin' into this world. Adren and I had twins on December 31, 1949. This birth was different than those that came before though. The midwife was there helpin' and said the baby was a-comin'. The first one came, and as she was takin' care of it, she turned around and the next one was comin' out, just a hand and a foot. I just imagine she was tryin' to turn the little one and broke its neck. She couldn't bring it to cry. They placed them in a diaper, one at a time, and hung them on the hand scales and they weighed about four pounds apiece. We named them Gary Lynn and Larry Gwen. Larry Gwen was the first child I had lost and, even though I never even knew the sound of that sweet one, I could feel emptiness within me.

At the same time, my 11-year-old son, Marvin, was ill and had appendicitis. The next day, we had the funeral for the twin and they sent Marvin to the hospital in Hugo, Oklahoma. He had been complainin' about his leg hurtin'. Some called it growin' pains, but instead it was the symptoms of his illness. Adren's sister Dell came over and they would go to see Marvin while he stayed there recoverin'. Seemed like it was five days that he had to stay in the hospital. It was a sad time. There I was with a little one to take care of and the other little kids. I didn't even get to go to the cemetery. They put a marker up, but my last visit over there we couldn't find it.

We did find a sense of normalcy there in the new house. I would do regular house keepin'. I had a Home Comfort cook stove with the firebox on the left, oven in the middle, and a five-gallon reservoir on the right. There was a warmin' closet up above the burners around the stovepipe for keepin' food warm. Adren made a bread pan out of a car door to just fit in the oven. I made thirty-six biscuits three times a day because Adren wouldn't eat cornbread.

We didn't have a television. We also worked our share of odd jobs. Me and the kids spent a couple of summers shakin' peanuts for John Vandever, a farmer about five miles from home. We would go over in the wagon and tie the team up. They'd plow the peanuts loose and have the workers pick them up, turn them upside down, shake the dirt off, and set them up towards the sky.

It was a snowy day the twenty-sixth of January 1951 when we added a new girl, named Sandra (Sandy), to the family after seven boys in a row. Sister (Beatrice) was thrilled and immediately cut Gary's long curls off. He was thirteen months old. I had gone to Antlers to stay with Adren's niece, Betty Ruth Smith, to be near the doctor who in housecoat and shoes, bag in hand, came just in time to hear her cry.

As we kept rollin' into the 1950s, nothin' much changed for us. Adren and the older kids found ways to help make ends meet. Sister, Marvin, and Calvin worked buddin' fruit trees for Thomas Gillum Wright in 1953. After that they, and Adren, went down to Texas and peeled pine poles, used for highline poles, for a couple of months.

A decade of stability came to an abrupt end as a result of Adren's drinkin', and our lives again took another direction. He pulled one drunk too many and was arrested. They took his driver's license and told him he had to buy insurance. It was somethin' like $300 that they wanted him to pay. Previously, he hadn't paid more than $20 when facin' a drunken charge. Instead of tryin' to get his license back and buyin' insurance, he came home and told me they took his driver's license and how much they wanted and said that he wouldn't pay it. He was movin' back to Arkansas. I had to sell the wagon, the team of mules, and Sister's horse she bought shakin' peanuts. In a couple days he took off durin' the night, drivin' his truck, to see his Uncle George in Montgomery County, Arkansas. In two or three weeks, he returned in middle of the night, roustin' us up and tellin' us "Get packed; we are goin' back to Arkansas." I hated to leave there. It was home to me. It was like the first time I left home all over again. You just get used to things, but I guess it's best not to.

It didn't take long to bring our belongin's together and load them in the truck bed. We put a partition between our stuff on one side and a space we made for my horse, Tony, to ride in on the other side of the truck bed. I had to ride with Tony to keep him comforted. Adren put a mattress on top of the dishes, cook stove and other belongin's. Part of the kids had to ride on that mattress — Sister (Beatrice), Marvin, Calvin, Russell, and R.G. The smallest — Eddie, Frog (Gary), and Sandy rode in the cab with their dad. After a while, Tony was settled in, and I was able to move into the cab with the little ones on my lap. As the moon shined down upon the road, breakin' the darkness of the night, I moved quietly out of Oklahoma, never to return to the home I had built there. As I held my youngest in my arms, I wondered what would be next; but I knew no matter where it might be or what was in store, it was just one more step in our journey together.

Adren, Violet, R.G., Beatrice, Marvin, Russell, and Calvin in
1945

Four horses with riders in Oklahoma in 1945 — From left are Evaline Peden on Sunshine (Adren's horse), with Jeannette Peden (her daughter) in front and Gene (her son) behind; Violet Hensley on Tony with R. G. in front and Bonnie, Evaline's daughter, behind; Bobby Skelton on her horse, Trigger, with her two children, George Henry and Linda, in front and Marvin Hensley (hidden) behind; and Beatrice Hensley on Dolly, with Russell in front and Calvin Hensley (hidden) behind.

Right: Adren Hensley wears his military uniform in 1944.

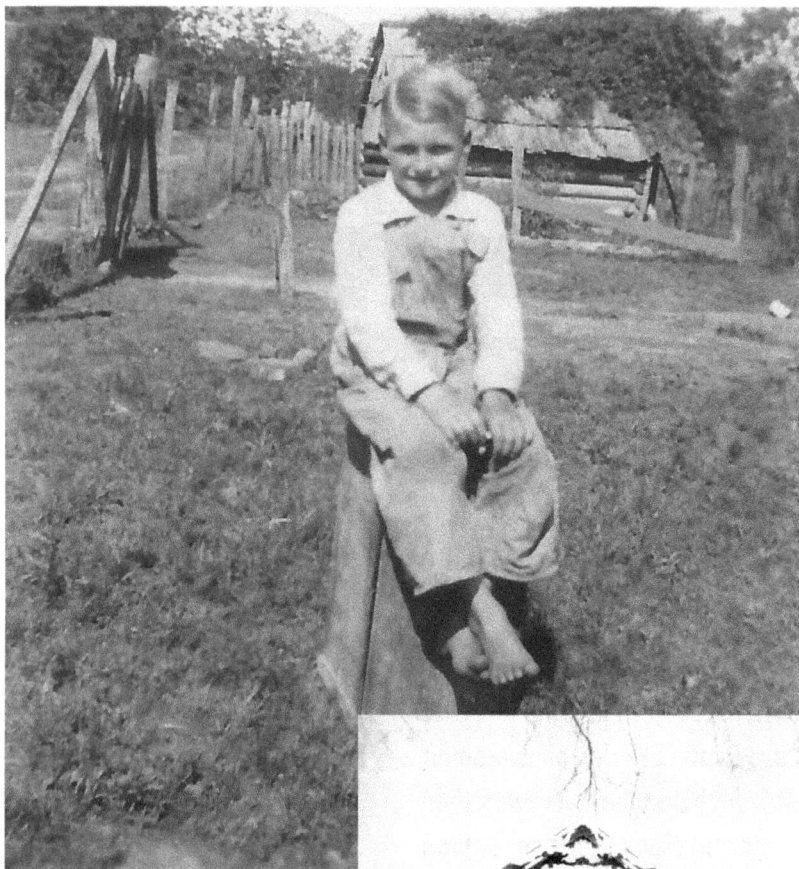

Marvin Hensley sits in front of the smokehouse on the Oklahoma farm in 1947.

Violet Hensley poses in Antlers, Oklahoma in 1946.

R. G. Hensley, George Washington "Wash" Brumley, Marvin Hensley, Russell
Hensley and Butch the dog gather on Wash's bench in 1947.

The shed and log barn at the Sobol, Oklahoma, farm in 1948. Thunder is seen
by the fence. Calvin was on him and was going to jump the gate.
Thunder stopped and Calvin didn't.

Russell Hensley (bottom left) pets a deer named Bucky as Beatrice Hensley, feeds Bucky. Eddie Hensley sits in Calvin Hensley's lap and Marvin Hensley stands by Bea's best friend, Vera Langley, in 1950.

Violet Hensley cuts Calvin Hensley's hair.

Violet Hensley rides Tony.

Left:
Adren
(left) and
Eddie
Hensley in
1949

Right:
Beatrice
Hensley
(right) and
Bonnie
Peden in
1945

Russell (left) and R.G. Hensley sit on the fenders of a
1931 Chevrolet cut down for a truck in 1946.

Back home in Arkansas and off to Oregon

Most of the kids found themselves able to doze into dreamland while we made our way through the night into Arkansas. It took us about two-and-half-hours to drive back to Hopper. That's where Adren had found a house for us to move into — one with a missin' board here and there and no electricity or water.

So we started yet again to make a new home. He got a job workin' with his brother-in-law, Bill Wehunt, cuttin' timber. We stayed in that house for about ten months before movin' into another vacant house that Ernest Cogburn owned, also in Hopper. We lived there for about four months. That was where Lewonna (Wonnie), our youngest, was born on November 8, 1954. We lived there for about six months.

An opportunity came to live rent-free in another house that belonged to Alvie Porter in January of 1955. This particular move would become important to one of my daughters, Sister, because she would meet, and later marry, a younger brother of Alvie's named Troy. We continued mak-ing memories there. That spring while at Alvie's place, I was plowin' the garden with Tony, and my five-year-old son, Gary, was followin' me. Suddenly he said, "When I get to be big, I'll be a big Frog, won't I?" Frog became his nickname. That same year he was followin' me along in the garden and he said, "Frogs lay eggs, but I don't, do I?"

That March, two weeks before R.G. turned eleven, he said he would chop wood all day long if I let him stay home from school. He cut wood in drizzly rain most of the day. Late in the afternoon, he started vomitin', and Adren was late gettin' in. We rushed him to Mount Ida to the doctor. The doctor thought it was acute appendicitis and told us to get him close to a hospital. R.G. had vomited eleven times by then. They took him right in and did surgery. They said it wasn't appendicitis but twisted intestines. The areas between the twists were as black as my coat. Had we been fifteen minutes later they couldn't have saved him. He was severely dehydrated and stayed in the hospital for a week. The next spring, the very same month, he came up hurtin' again. We rushed him back to the hospital. This time they removed three feet of his intestines. He turned twelve in the hospital durin' his two-week stay.

We made some good memories, too. Sister graduated from Caddo Gap School and got a job. She came in one evenin' and took me to town, and when we got there, she told me I was goin' to buy a gas stove or walk the twelve miles back home. So, I made a downpayment on my first butane cook stove.

We stayed at Alvie's until December 1956, and then, once again, we were chasin' greener pastures across the country. This time it was Oregon that was the shinin' place of hope for our future. My youngest sister, Evaline, was out there workin' in the harvest, and she wrote me sayin', "With all your kids' here workin' with you, you would get rich." Sister and Marvin were the first to decide to go. Sister was datin' Troy who was already out there workin' in another town where he could come and visit. She left on August 26, 1956, and Marvin followed in November. Each one had traveled by bus to Monmouth, Oregon.

Adren thought it over, as well, and decided he would sell our Oklahoma farm that we had abandoned in 1953 and we would move to Oregon. So he went back, sold it, and returned with $1,500 in his pocket. He had seen a school bus for sale nearby, and he went and bought it. All of the seats had been taken out except the driver's seat and the first passenger seat on the right side where I rode. We put dishes in my mother's wash pot and the number four fiddle in her small trunk behind the passenger seat. By that time I had to can a lot to feed a family of eleven, and I had canned five bushels of peaches as well as other fruits and vegetables. All these went in boxes in the floor in the back of the bus with a few boxes of other household goods. They were stacked high enough that when the mattresses were placed on top of them side by side, they were about level with the bottom of the windows. That's where the kids rode.

The sewin' machine and my brand new gas cook stove went agin the left-hand side between the beds and driver. Although that's the biggest vehicle we ever moved in, I still wasn't able to take my new refrigerator or our bedsteads. Also, Tony couldn't make this trip, so he became a guest of Sheriff Tidwell, who kept him free so his twelve-year-old could use him — and he just loved Tony. Wonnie cried so much over leavin' Tony, that we bought her a little rubber horse that looked the most like Tony. She was crazy about ridin' that horse.

It took three days to get to Monmouth, Oregon, and on the second day in Arizona, near Needles, California, the fuel pump went out. Adren caught a ride into Needles and got a replacement. The kids and I stayed with the bus. It was cold and the boys were scroungin' around lookin' for sticks to make a fire to keep us warm when Russell found a rusty, ragged, five-dollar bill. It was wrapped around a stick inside a crumbly, rusty, can. Part of it was missin', and it had to be handled very carefully. After Adren got back and fixed the bus, we made it into Needles where Russell exchanged it for a good five-dollar bill. Five dollars would buy a lot back then. On the third day, we stopped at a gas station in Myrtle Creek, Oregon. Everyone got out to go to the restroom and got back in again. We had gone only a little way when a cop pulled us over and said, "You left one of your crew behind." Frog, our almost seven-year-old, because his feet were cold, had still been in the restroom when we left. It took a while to find a place big enough to turn that big old bus around, but we eventually made it back. Frog was waitin' patiently for us, but he was glad to get back on the bus.

We arrived at my sister's just before Christmas. They had found us a house nearby in Independence, Oregon. It was our first and only two-story house with both runnin' water and electricity. Not only that, it had a modern bathtub and a flushin' toilet. Adren got a job at a metal refinery to work until the next harvest. He was injured when hot metal went in the top of his shoe and he couldn't wear shoes for a while. By the time he got well, strawberries came in, and we went to pickin'.

While Sandy, and Wonnie didn't work because they were too young, the rest did, all day, everyday, until the tasks were done. We just moved from crop to crop as they came in, pickin' beans, cherries, filberts, prunes, whatever was in season. In the fall after pickin' filberts, Adren and I went to Klamath Falls, Oregon, and Tule Lake, California, and picked up taters for several weeks before the big harvest. We left the kids in Independence with Sister. After returnin' to Independence, we all went to Avondale,

Arizona, and picked cotton for a couple of months in November and December. Sister left for Arkansas from Arizona where she married Troy Porter on December 31, 1957. We finished the harvest season in Arizona and headed back to Oregon.

We repeated these steps the next year, but left Oregon intendin' to stop in Arizona to pick cotton then continue to Arkansas. Someone had told us about forty acres available for $250 in Marion County, Arkansas, so I had told Adren we were goin' back there. He agreed that he was ready to go back, too. Unlike what my sister had said in her letter, we did not get rich in Oregon. We made pretty good. We had $400 dollars that we had saved up and had to use it to work on the engine of the bus so we could return to Arkansas. We initially landed in Brinkley, after a brief visit with Sister and Troy on the way, because we had brought another worker we met called Poor Harry back with us. His name was Harry Simons, but everyone just called him Poor Harry. He had a place in Brinkley where we stayed about two months.

We all moved up to Yellville, on February 9, 1959. Poor Harry stayed in Yellville with us about two months and then went on back to Oregon. We found out that the real estate man had sold his last forty acres for $250, but we bought forty acres for $500 and another eighty for $1,700. Adren cut and sold timber off the forty, and we eventually sold the land as well. Right off, we moved into an old shack on the eighty-acre farm. Oh my, that place, it was so black. Everything was black and dirty. The refrigerator was a year old, and it was moldy. I asked the woman that owned it where she got her water, and she said out of the cistern for drinkin' and cookin' and if you wasn't too particular, out of the pond to wash with. She was leavin' when they brought us in. She took her clothes and left everything else. The cistern was a concrete-walled hole in the ground with a well curb and hand pump. Rain drained off the roof through a gutter into it. I couldn't bring myself to drink out of it. We had three metal cream cans; two ten-gallon cans and a five-gallon can that we kept water in inside the bus.

We had to clean the house up good. We stayed in the school bus for a couple of days. It took us that long to clean it. We found a pile of sheets and hand towels; enough to fill a small pickup truck. Initially, we began burnin' them because they were so black. I got to lookin', and we decided to boil and wash them. It turned out we had some nice white sheets, pillowcases, and towels. The dishes were all filthy, too. Eventually, we got the house cleaned up enough to move in. I had to go back to cookin' with wood on the wood cook stove that was in the kitchen because we had no butane. We put our bed in the livin' room and slept there with the girls on the old couch. The boys slept on the boarded up porch. It came a cold spell, and we had to put all the extra blankets, quilts, and even coats, on the boys' beds. They woke up one mornin' with ice on their brows and the front of their hair from their breathin'.

After Adren sold the timber off those forty acres, he went to work for Bill Madden. Adren drove a bus from Yellville to Marshall, haulin' workers to the shirt factory. In the spring, Calvin got a job with Bill Madden haulin' strawberries to Springfield, and me and the kids picked strawberries for $.03 a quart. Adren poured a concrete slab and added two new rooms to the house — a bedroom for Adren and me and a new kitchen. The girls' bedroom was moved to the old kitchen. One day, a mule wandered into the yard with a collar sign on its neck, and I knew it had been worked. A harness and plows were left in the sheds, so I harnessed the mule and used it to break the garden. Some women came by and asked whose mule I was usin', and I said I didn't know. It turned out it was Loy Shipman's mule. He was surprised that I caught him because he was normally hard to catch. I borrowed a horse to finish the garden.

The next year, we went to get Tony and bought a big mule we called old Blue. We could take Blue to the woods and hook him to a log and have him drag it where we wanted it. After that, we would go and get another log, wrap the lines on the hames out of his way, and send him back alone. If he hit a stump, with the log, he'd pull one way, then the other, till he got loose. He pulled the log right up beside the others 'til he thought the ends were even, and then he would stop. We unhooked him and sent him back for another.

The kids had to walk a mile-and-a-half to catch the bus. We had to get the doctor to say R.G. couldn't be walkin' that far in all kinds of weather everyday so the bus would finally come to the end of our drive. Russell graduated in 1960 and went right into the Navy, then into the Army. Twenty years later, he retired from the Army. In September, Calvin moved to California where he and Marvin made their home.

Things were tight in 1961, and I told the kids we didn't have money for Christmas gifts. Frog was almost twelve and didn't want to believe it. He woke up first before daylight and started to make a fire. He thought the fire was completely out. There was an empty gas can I had emptied to wash my paintbrushes with next to the front door. Evidently it had enough in it that the stove exploded when Frog poured it on the wood in the stove. The girls were in bed on the other side of the wall from the stove. That was about the time of the Cuban bomb scare. Adren had been talkin' about it lately. When the stove exploded, Wonnie, who had just turned six, jumped out of the bed into the doorway and was jumpin' up and down screamin', "It's a bomb! It's a bomb!" Someone either sent her outside or carried her. Adren grabbed Sandy out of the bed and took her outside. Someone else put a broom in her hand and told her to start helpin' beat out the flames, but she just stood there beatin' the ground tryin' to wake up. Frog was runnin' 'round and 'round the house. He had singed all the hair off his face, but was otherwise unhurt. It cracked the windows, scorched the sewin' machine cabinet, and curled a large souvenir comb that had hung on the wall by the door. The boys' jackets hung on the wall to the side of the stove, and they were burned. The ceilin' caught on fire, but with everyone helpin', we quickly put it out. The inside of the livin' room was damaged, but we were thankful the house did not burn down. The neighbors gave the boys new coats, and Mr. Palmateer brought about a dishpan full of hard candy for the kids' Christmas.

In 1962 when I was forty-six, I decided to get my driver's license. Adren bought me a 1955 blue and white Chevrolet. We became a two-car family for the first time. I had a driver's license way back before you had to take a test. You just went in and bought one, but Adren always did the drivin'. I had a sick spell — a bad cold in November. I took cold pills and used Vicks VapoRub ® and got over it. I got a letter invitin' me to a fiddler's contest somewhere in the winter of 1964, and I decided whether I entered it or not I could go listen to them. Because I hadn't played much for so long, I wasn't good enough to enter, I thought. The very next day, Wilma Kyles, our neighbor, and a nurse at the hospital, came by and asked if I wanted to go to work at the hospital. I went in and applied for the job, and they said, "You know you have four others ahead of you, but come back Monday." As soon as I walked in, they said, "Are you ready to go to work? You sound like the one most likely to stay with the job." I didn't have a uniform, but I went right to work in the kitchen on December 29. I worked about three years in the kitchen, and then went to housekeepin'. I worked there for fifteen years.

I continued havin' about five of those sick spells before and after I started work. I was so weak. At the hospital, the handle on the dishwasher had to be held through the rinse cycle for it to work, but it was so hard to do in my weakened condition. I'd go to the bathroom and cry and think, "I can't do this. I gotta quit." Then I'd think, "I gotta stay." I couldn't quit because we were five payments behind on the property. I weighed about 100 pounds. My neighbor insisted in February on that fifth spell that I go to the doctor. The doctor said I had walkin' pneumonia. He gave me medicine and told me to stay in bed three days. I was already scheduled to be off two days, and on the third day I went to work. I got two meals a day at work, and I gradually recovered.

I saw Mr. Palmateer downtown about April. He said, "Mrs. Hensley, I'm glad to see you lookin' better. I tell you right now I didn't think you would make it through the winter." Even though Adren had fallen those five payments behind, on the land, Mr. Palmateer had never dunned us or even mentioned it. Workin' at the hospital, I was able to catch up on the payments and get our first phone and television set. Later Adren got mad at someone on TV and shot the TV. Since we were both workin' in town, we decided to leave our place on the Bruno-Ridge Road and rent a place in Yellville in the summer of 1965. We would have cold runnin' water and a flushin' toilet again with a galvanized washtub for a bathtub.

Our son, R.G., had graduated in 1963 and went to live with Sister and work with Troy in the woods. Then he went to South Dakota to work at a sawmill. He had bought about a five-acre wooded parcel of land right at the city limits of Yellville from Mr. Palmateer. He bought a truck so, we made a deal with him and Mr. Palmateer. We traded the eighty acres on Bruno Ridge Road for R.G.'s property. I got an FHA* loan to build a house, and construction began on our first modern home since the first two years we lived in Oregon. We moved in October of 1968. We were then close to the hospital and grocery store, and while I didn't know it at the time, it would be where I would spend the rest of my life.

Music found its way back into our lives oncet we settled back into Arkansas. Before we got married, my dad and I played for dances. Adren use to say he had two wrong feet, but actually he was just jealous. He didn't want anybody else to look at me, so I stopped playin' for twenty-seven years except occasionally for my own pleasure. People found out I played the fiddle some, and they would say, "Bring your fiddle," when they invited us over. Adren got his guitar out and we got to playin' again. Later, we got acquainted with Ray and Obeda Fisk. Ray played the fiddle, and Obeda played the bass and guitar. Their two boys also played guitars. They often wanted us to come out to their house or they come to ours. We would just sit around and play tune after tune, havin' what they call now a jam session. Then we got in with other friends who moved

* Federal Housing Administration loans began being offered in 1934.

from Louisiana — Ralph and Arlis Vines. Ralph was a good guitar player, and they were both good singers. Through the years, there were many local friends we made through music. Archie Truax was a left-hander, and I fixed him a fiddle up and taught him to play Faded Love. His wife was named Ruby. Herman and Alice McCrory didn't play music but often hosted events, and Ray Queen played the mandolin.

In the fall of 1959, Russell took my fiddle to show at school. He came home tellin' us about the Turkey Trot Festival in Yellville. I made fiddle number five in 1961 and played it at Turkey Trot in October 1961 where I met Jimmy Driftwood. Adren and I and the girls would often load up and head down to Mountain View where Jimmy Driftwood had music goin' on at the courthouse on Fridays and Saturdays. Sometime later, he had a fiddler named Parks in from Nashville who played my number five fiddle and loved it so much; he took it on stage with him even though three or four other fiddlers offered him theirs. We enjoyed the visits down at Mountain View watchin' the music and doin' a little pickin' with friends. As I watched the players on stage, I never really saw myself as a performer. No matter where you see yourself in life though, the path you see may be shadowed by the trees you have grown to shade your life and make it comfortable. You never know when a big wind will come along and reveal an unseen fork in the road for you.

The Hensley Family gathers at the 2nd Street house in Independence, Oregon, on July 4, 1957. From left are Adren, Marvin, Calvin, Russell, Beatrice, R.G., Eddie, Gary, Sandra, Lewonna, and Violet.

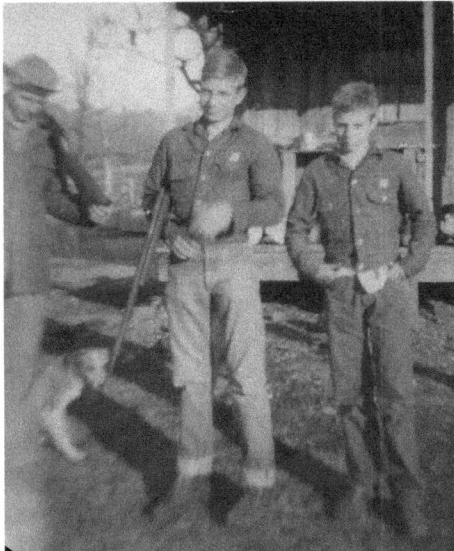

Marvin, Calvin, and Russell Hensley
go hunting at Knold's Place.

Violet Hensley (left) with Lewonna and Violet's sister Dorothy with her son James in 1955.

Russell, R.G., and Gary (Frog) Hensley in 1955, at Knold's place in Hopper, Arkansas.

Tony giving Violet Hensley a kiss.

Bright lights and microphones

Except for the rhythmic sounds that I helped create for square dances as a youth and for livin' room gatherin's, I had never stepped up on a stage in front of people to play until one fateful day in 1962. For years, I had been busy with raisin' a family and keepin' us fed. I guess in a way it was my children that drew me onto the stage. The Yellville Summit School was hostin' a talent show as part of the Turkey Trot. Turkey Trot is an annual town event where when it first started, turkeys were dropped from an airplane, and kids tried to catch a turkey. I remember one time when one got stuck in a tree at the courthouse. You should have seen the kids tryin' to get up the tree to get it. Two of my children did get a turkey back then. One caught a live one, and another won one from a drawin'.

I wasn't even thinkin' about enterin' the contest until Sue Evans and another schoolteacher came to see me askin' me to enter. I didn't know whether I should or not. I liked playin', but in many ways I was still that little bashful girl from Alamo. Eventually I took my fiddle up town and stopped in the grocery store on the square and played the tunes I was thinkin' about for Mrs. Clem. I asked her which I should play in the contest. She picked the "Eighth of January."

In anticipation of the day, I pulled out some feed sacks I was savin' and made me a dress to wear. It was blue with yellow and red flowers. I also made new dresses for the two girls, Sandy and Wonnie, and two shirts for Eddie and Frog to wear to the contest. The night came, and we rode up to the Yellville school gym. When we got there, you couldn't stir the people with a stick. There must have been more than 200 folks there. There were thirty-two contestants signed up. Some performed skits. Some recited poems. The Shipman Girls sang a song called "Itsy Bitsy Teeny Weeny Yellow Polkadot Bikini." Dennis Fisk was one of the fiddlers competin'.

When it came my turn, I was scared to death as I walked in front of that mic and looked out at all those people. I just had to draw within myself and look at the fiddle and start playin' the "Eighth of January." I didn't have a back-up musician. My husband wouldn't back me up back then. It was just me facin' the crowd. As I finished, the gym filled with applause and cheers. When I stepped off the stage I was still nervous despite the crowd's reception — so much so it made my back hurt all night. When it was said and done I took third place and won $15.

After the experience, I wondered sometime how I ever walked on stage again. I don't know that it gave me the desire to get on stage any-more, but I had people get after me to come and play. Never bein' one to back down, I did. I guess I got a little braver 'cause people told me even the best players make mistakes, and eventually I also started playin' pic-nics at Buffalo River Park.

One area I never seemed to make mistakes was with animals. They just took to me. And in a way, that love led to me taking on a whole dif-ferent kind of performin'. Well, at least it offered me the opportunity to present another talent to add to the performin' I was doin'. Wild things just seemed to make themselves at home around me, whether it was a deer, or even a pet squirrel that came around in 1962. I could open my hand, turn it face up, curl my fingers up, and tap on the floor with the back of my hand and that squirrel, called Baby, would come tearin' across the floor and ball up on my hand. It acted ferocious, but didn't ever hurt me. However, Baby would meet Adren at the door, jump on one of his shoulders, bite his ear, switch to the other side, and bite that ear as he tried to swat her. Then she'd jump off and be gone before he could hit her. Baby was allowed to run free in '63. She left for a short time, came back for about two months, then didn't return. She built a nest in the woods with some of our household items in it. Adren found Baby and the nest eventually.

I guess it was my love of animals that inspired me so much to start carvin' them out of wood. I was most comfortable when I had wood and a knife in my hand creatin' a fiddle or somethin' else out of the wood I was holdin'. My favorite pocket knife came with a pair of jeans I bought for the boys, probably around 1950. It now forms a point shaped by the thousands of strokes my hands have pushed and pulled with it across hundreds of pieces of bass, soft maple, myrtle, cherry, buckeye, and walnut. Even though it is my favorite, I have probably worn out twenty-five Old Timer, Camillus, and other pocket knives to complete the close to 2,500 animals that have taken shape by my hands. This knife came from beneath the muck of the old pond on our property, lost by one of my boys when they were playin'. I had brought it up workin' with a road slip behind the horse and cleaned it up. A lot of folks do not realize you can stick a good knife in dirt for six months and the blade will be better to work with. I have never been able to do much with stainless steel though; I can't keep a good edge on it.

My fascination with wood began as a child workin' beside my father helpin' him make the practical things that we used everyday — handles for hammers, saws, and even a gunstock. I was so clean with my pocket knife that the teacher would have me sharpen all the pencils at school since we did not have a sharpener. Eventually, watchin' my dad's woodworkin' would lead to me makin' myself a heart-shaped jewelry box of bass wood and startin' on fiddle makin', but I never gave up whittlin'. As the years passed, I found it to be somethin' I could do to pass the time between supper and bedtime. I would pull out a piece a wood and begin shavin' off until I saw what the wood was holdin' within it. One of the first lastin' pieces I carved was a flat-faced wooden doll I made in the 1930s. I made it with the wavy hair lookin' like women wore in the 1920s with a wave goin' all the way around. I made its arms move and fastened the arms and legs on with a piece of copper wire. I loved horses, so my first animal to carve was a baby colt.

My work creatin' what is now considered wood folk art didn't really take off until 1956 when we were on our way to Oregon. As we drove along Route 66, in the window of one of the many gas stations that we stopped at was a lamp shaped like a covered wagon with horses in front of it. Oncet I saw that, I got in my mind I could make one. In the night hours while we were workin' in Oregon, I began the project, findin' the pieces of pinewood I needed. I finished, and it looked just like the one I saw, so I carried it back with us as we returned to Arkansas. While we were stopped pickin' cotton in Arizona, someone saw it and asked if I would sell it. I did for twenty-five dollars. I went on to make a couple more of those covered wagon lamps, sellin' them as well. Creatin' those got me interested in carvin' more horses. I had spent my life around horses like my Tony; I could see the wood would make a horse real easy. I just had to shave off the extra wood. If you made a horse like it was walkin', they were harder to carve than if the legs were standin' even.

I found a picture of Roy Rogers' Trigger and used it to create a seven- or eight-inch soft maple Trigger. One time Roy Rogers Jr. came to the City, and I took Trigger out to show him. He seemed impressed by how I had really caught him in the wood. I also carved a soft maple image of my Tony. The biggest I ever carved was a rearin' horse in walnut, and I think I sold it for about $14. One time, I saw a chocolate Easter rabbit and thought I would try to carve one of those — and then I started dogs, geese, buffalos, and horse heads. I had twenty-three different designs for pins to wear on your clothes (brooches) — duck, cats, fiddles, and many more. After the first few pieces I made, I signed "VH" to the back of the pins and bottom of the carvin's.

Through the years, I collected pictures of animals from magazines and cut them out to create a paper pattern. After pickin' what kind of wood I wanted to use for a carvin', I outlined the shape on the wood with a pencil usin' the pattern. With a saw, I blocked out the wood. Then is when the whittlin' would start by takin' out the parts that were not needed. Through the years, I built a collection of pocket knives that I used for whittlin' various parts of a project, beginnin' with a two-inch blade for the initial stages and gettin' smaller blades as I got down to fine finishin' with legs, tails, nose, and eyes of the animals. One time I was sent an old piece of worm-eaten myrtle wood. There were more holes than wood. I worked for hours to carefully whittle a Rhodesian Ridgeback dog. I worked hard to not break the wood. You have to have a very sharp knife to cut against the grain and not break a leg or tail off a carvin'. It is still one of my favorite pieces.

I liked workin' with harder woods because they smoothed out better, makin' pretty slick and shiny carvin's. After I sanded them smooth, I applied a coat of True Oil to preserve the color of the wood. This is the same stuff I used when finishin' a gunstock. I made just about every kind of gunstock workin' with Adren for his guns and occasionally for someone else. I would help carve out the trigger guard pockets.

After a while of makin', at the suggestion of my friend Freda Snipes, I decided to try my hand at sellin' these at one of the bigger craft fairs we had in Arkansas — War Eagle. I sent them a sample of a little dog I carved out of Cocobolo wood in 1965. They wrote and said to come on and set up. I prepared a bunch of my little pins and some carvin's in the round of geese, horses, and dogs and brought my number five fiddle to show. I worked on number six at the event.

As I started doin' craft shows, I would get requests from folks to carve. For example, a doctor once ordered two Brahma bulls; a man from Kansas sent me a picture of his Collie. Frogs were harder than horses for me, but the hardest of all was a buffalo. War Eagle was held in October in a big field by War Eagle Creek nestled next to an old gristmill. Craft people set up their tents and tables and, as folks milled around, they would work and talk to folks about what they were doin'. I would also do a little fiddlin' to catch folks' attention as they browsed. I sold the little pins I made for seventy-five cents apiece and the carvin's for up to four dollars. I did pretty good the first year, so I decided to go back in 1966 and do it again. That decision to go to a craft show changed the direction of where my talents and my life would go.

While browsin' through War Eagle in 1966, Don Richardson, a marketin' representative from Silver Dollar City — an amusement park in Branson, Missouri — stopped by and visited. I didn't know who he was; he was just someone else interested in what I was doin'. I had never heard of Silver Dollar City. Don didn't mention it to me either. Freda suggested I might go to Silver Dollar City, so I decided to load up my children after War Eagle and visit. It didn't cost to get in there then. As we walked through the park, a man walked up to me and talked to me like he knew me. It was Don, and he asked me if I had received his letter. I hadn't yet, but it was there when I got home. Don wanted me to come and demonstrate fiddle makin' at Silver Dollar City durin' the Fall Festival. I agreed, and decided to go there the next year instead of to War Eagle. Without a day at the City under my belt, I was surprised in the summer of 1967 when Don came along with Mary and Pete Herschend and their photographer Gary Gillam, and asked me to join their main group of crafters that worked to raise awareness about the City. This meant that I would travel with the group and share my talents on television and radio and with newspaper reporters in cities around the country. I hadn't known much else but the farms we worked, the little towns we lived in, and a few years worth of craft fairs. This was a big step for me. All of a sudden my little fiddle makin' craft table with a handful of folks standin' about was gettin' ready to open shop in front of millions of dedicated TV viewers, radio listeners, and newspaper readers. I wondered to myself whether I could even do it.

Don asked me how the proposal sounded, and I replied "Sounds OK, but I don't know if I can do the talk or not." I just didn't know enough about the City at that point to be able to carry on a conversation about it. They thanked me and went on back. I received a letter lettin' me know that joinin' their main team had not worked out but they would be back in touch later. Don wrote me to come and bring my fiddle makin' in the fall.

As my first season at the City neared in 1967, I was a little bit anxious. I guess it was sort of like that feelin' I had when I waited to go on stage back at the school, but I busied myself with preparin'. The City paid me by the day to be there and demonstrate makin' the fiddle — and of course while doin' it playin' what I made as folks gathered up around me. My first season at Silver Dollar City took a different approach than the other craft fair I did. To begin with, I had to step back into the 1880s. All crafts people at the City dress to fit the standards of this period. I had made my dresses throughout my life, so there ain't much different about that except now I was makin' a dress closer to what my mother and grandmother wore with the bonnet. The first long dress I made was gray with little black square designs in it. It had long sleeves and a high neck, and I made a matchin' bonnet. With it I wore black socks and black shoes. The first season I made three dresses and bonnets — the others were one that was brown with polka dots and blue print one. I brought only one completed fiddle and one fiddle underway to show. This would be my first time to tell visitors how I built fiddles.

I rented a little cabin near the City to stay in at night and traveled the seventy-five miles on Sunday. That first Monday I had to be in the Gazebo ready to show at 8 a.m. and would stay there until 6 p.m. The festival was sixteen days long, and it rained nine days, but not in a row.

My first display area was a table one employee at the City made for me about two feet long, one foot wide and eighteen inches high. One of the first things I faced as I stood there and folks would stop by is that some would ask, "What kind of wood does he use in his fiddles?" I guess they assumed that only men could make fiddles. I would quickly reply sayin', "He doesn't use any kind of wood — I do. I make these fiddles." For quite a while it seemed I was rowin' upstream tryin' to get folks to understand that fiddle makin' is somethin' that a woman could and would do. After breakin' the ice though, I would soon have them interested in how I did what I did rather than the fact I was a woman. I had never really thought of their bein' much difference between men and women workin' before that. On the farm, with two hands and two legs, off you went to get whatever needin' doin' done. I often had men say to my dad, "She can wield an ax as well any man." That was the first time I seemed to encounter outsiders' perceptions about what women did or didn't do. Though I was doin' somethin' that I didn't know any other women did, I did want opportunities in work to be available for all my girls and my boys, especially the youngest who were still goin' through school.

Except on the rainy days, there was a steady stream of folks visitin' to see the Marvel Cave and the crafts. The cave, previously called Marble Cave, initially was discovered by the Osage Indians and by the late 1800s was a place for adventurers and miners. Canadian mining expert William Lynch made it the focus of public tours beginning in 1894. The Herschends, Silver Dollar City founders, leased the cave from his daughters.

There were many crafts — leather, spinnin' and weavin', candle makin', pottery, dulcimer makin', chair canein', broom makin', rope makin', and soap makin'. Regular crafters at the City included a blacksmith and a glass blower. Folks could also buy ice cream and possibly candy. I had a partner in the Gazebo that first few days from Lynn McSpadden Dulcimers. Almost every person who came up to me wanted to hear me play the fiddle, and, of course, the same was true for the dulcimer. It wasn't long before the City realized we didn't quite complement each other and decided to move the dulcimer to another location.

I made the trip back home on Friday and picked up Adren, Sandy, and Wonnie, and we would return and perform in the Gazebo together Saturday and Sunday. One of the men who came to listen took the bait when I asked if he knew what this was — holdin' up the jawbone from a horse that I was playin' at the time. He replied "You think I have been a cowboy for sixty years and don't know what a horse's jawbone is?" Then I furthered my question with "What kind?" and he said, "You mean what nationality? … Looks like it might be a pony." I agreed sayin', "Yeah, It's a Shetland."

As the time drew to a close, in a way although I was tired, I hated to see it end. Unlike goin' on stage to play a tune one time, at these types of craft fairs, you are on stage from the time you walk in your booth until the time you leave. You just vary what you're doin' as the day goes on. Your audience can range from one to as many as could crowd in to ear- and eye-shot.

Then, five years after my stage fright, I was growin' to enjoy what I was doin'. This stage allowed me to be me and not be that concerned about puttin' on a show. I just did what I did, said what I said, played what I played, and whittled what I wanted. When I asked Don much later what drew him to me, he answered, "a little personality goes a long ways." I guess that sums it up — that's what folks have told the survey-takers at the City through the years as my name appeared over and over. They said they liked my personality.

Violet and Adren Hensley play at Buffalo River National Park in
St. Joe, Arkansas, in 1961. She plays her number four fiddle.

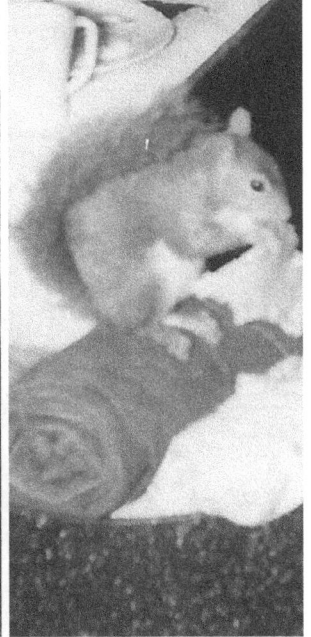

Left: Blue is carrying Lewonna, Sandra, Gary, Pat Devore, Eddie, and R.G.
with Violet Hensley at Blue's side in 1961. Right: Baby, the squirrel

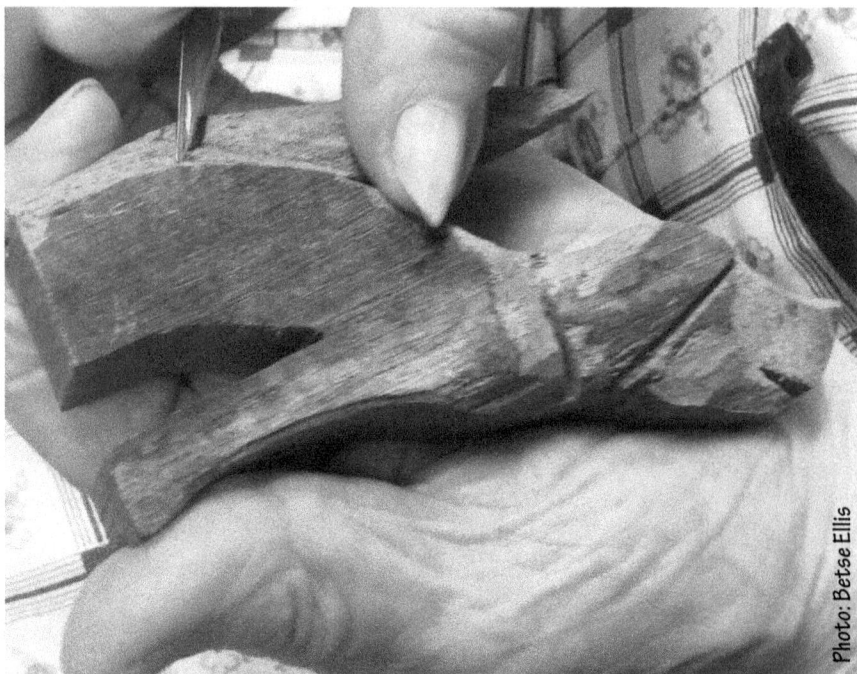

Violet
Hensley
carves
a dog.

Photo: Betse Ellis

Photo: Marion Fenix

Violet Hensley shows her number five (1961) (left) and number four (1934) fiddles in 1962.

Violet Hensley and the kids; from left, Lewonna, Sandra, R. G., Violet, and Gary, sell huckleberries in 1962.
"We ate 'em, canned 'em, and sold 'em."

Violet's children show off her garden on
Bruno Ridge Road filled with mustard greens in 1963.

Violet Hensley performs with Sandra and Adren Hensley
at Silver Dollar City in 1967.

Silver Dollar City performers, from left are (front) Violet Hensley, Art
Galbraith, Manuel Wood, (back) By Kelly, Chick Allen, Lewonna Hensley, Sandra
Hensley, Adren Hensley, Jude Herndon, and Thelma Wood in 1968.

A reluctant star

With one year under my belt at Silver Dollar City, I knew more about it and could share the experience. As organizers made plans for the 1968 season, I was included among the main group of crafters and would travel to promote what the City was about. I signed papers with the City allowin' people to use my picture and name as part of the promotions. My first promotional tour would be over seven weeks in a row. I'd get home on Saturday or Sunday and be gone again Monday through Friday.

The opportunity presented me with the first time in my life I would travel extensively by myself without another family member. I was goin' to leave Adren and my youngest girls behind at home to fend for themselves for the first time in my life. While you might think I would have had some worries about this, amazingly, I didn't. The girls were old enough to look after themselves and get to school. Adren could cook when he got hungry, if the girls didn't cook somethin' he wanted. I had full confidence in them takin' care of things, and they didn't seem to mind me goin' off. Adren and I were at a point in our relationship so different from those early years when his jealousy pulled me away from playin' my music at dances. Now we were both in our fifties and tryin' to make ends meet. Adren was workin' for a company doin' black toppin' on parkin' lots and fixin' cars. My work for the City provided an opportunity that was unexpected but at the same time provided a couple of hundred dollars each week to help us. Now, Adren was glad we had the music and the fiddle makin' because of the opportunity for the money I earned.

I wanted to make sure that as I traveled I could remember where I had been so I could tell Adren and the family about my adventures when I called or returned home. I hadn't ever written a diary, so I decided to take little notepads along on my trips and I would just jot down random thoughts and experiences that at the time I wanted to remember. It is amazin' to me some of the simple things at the time I wanted to remember that really mean little now, while I wish I had written more about things I now see as significant. These travels described in the comin' chapters reflect some of the people and places from my notepads.

I was still a little nervous about goin' — not of goin' on TV or radio but of goin' on an airplane. They had told me I would have to fly on some of the trips. That is what set my fifty-one-year-old heart to racin'. To start with, I was able to keep both feet firmly planted on the ground — that is, on the floorboard of Peter Engler's station wagon. My very first trip began with me drivin' to the City on September 3, 1968 and crawlin' into the station wagon headed to St. Louis, Missouri, with Pete and an indian that couldn't sit up straight if he tried. He was dead to the world. When a policeman pulled us over along the way, I wondered what he might say about the Indian's body in the back. Pete was stopped because he was drivin' on a car tag that expired by a month. To my surprise, our friend in the back just laid there the whole time, unnoticed by the police officer. You see, the Indian was one of Pete's creations made out of sassafras wood. He had sold it to a feller up there in St. Louis and after we delivered it, we met the rest of the crew at the motel.

Among the crew were Don Richardson, the PR man for Silver Dollar City. We called him our "get-lost leader." He couldn't drive anywhere without gettin' lost. One time when we went to O'Hara Airport in Chicago, he got in one car and we got in another. We made it and he got lost. He got lost drivin' one time from Fort Worth to Dallas, Texas. Also on this trip was Pete Herschend, (brother to Jack Herschend and son of Hugo and Mary Herschend, who started the park); Ethel Huffman, our lye soap maker; and Lloyd "Shad" Heller, our blacksmith.

My road to television stardom began on Wednesday, September 4, 1968, as the camera lights were brought up on "Corky's Colorama" at KSD-TV (NBC) in St. Louis. I will never forget the first time I walked into a television studio. I came out from behind a dark black curtain. My first sight was these large cords trailin' across the floor attached to the huge television cameras. Behind each was a man in tow. There were bright lights that shined down from the ceilin' highlightin' the colorful makeup worn by the host of my first show.

Cliff St. James was Corky the Clown. I didn't get many chances to see clowns close up like, and he sure was a good-lookin' clown. For St. Louis children, he uplifted and taught them many lessons that would stick with them through their lives. As I look back, I laugh and wonder sometimes if the experiences of standin' side by side with so many television clowns had any impact on how I shared what I did. I think I learned a little bit of presence from each of them. Corky was friendly with me and carin' with his young audience. He put me at ease quickly and before I knew it, the camera cords, and the lights had just melted away into the darkness as the two of us just talked about makin' fiddles. Soon, I was playin' for the folks at home.

Throughout the years, the approach that my City companions and I came to have in presentin' on television was much the same, dependin' upon who was along for the tour. I would talk a little about the fiddle makin' and then would play a little bit. They would want to talk more about what other kind of crafts they could see at the City. Those of us along would split up different aspects to talk about, whether it was black-smithin', rope makin', dyein' and spinnin' thread, or chair makin'. You did not give the audience too much, just enough for them to want to come to Silver Dollar City.

The next day on that first trip brought us to KMOX-TV (CBS) for my second show. It was across from the Gateway Arch — the so-called Gateway to the West — in St. Louis. Some of the group went up in the elevator on it, I had never been in one of those things before and I didn't have any hankerin' to try it.

That afternoon was followed with an appearance on KSD radio with Pete Herschend, Shad, and me. That show marked my first experience of becomin' a classical music performer or playin' with a large group of musicians. The show was already broadcastin', and we stepped into a radio studio and I sat down in front of a thirty-piece orchestra that includ-ed brass, strings, percussion, woodwinds, and piano. I played my fiddle with Shad by my side givin' his best performance on a handsaw. We kicked it off, and we were surprisingly in tune with them. The orchestra joined us for an amazin' rendition of "Turkey in the Straw."

After becomin' more uptown with the orchestra, I had to then become more up close and personal with the clouds as we headed for the airport.

When I arrived for my very first experience on a plane, let's just say I was wishin' I had my hammer so I could nail my shoe soles to the ground. Needless to say though, I was quickly urged to join the rest of the group inside the plane. I was greeted by our pilot, Ted Vrizzius, who was very nice. The others just took it in stride and made themselves comfortable while I felt like a fish out of water. It was a nine-passenger Cessna we were travelin' in. After we took off, you could hardly tell we were goin' anywhere. The others were just talkin' or restin', and I was wonderin' how high we were and when the ground would be under my shoes again. That didn't keep my curiosity from drawin' my eyes to the windows to look below at the ground.

I remember that we ran into a heavy storm on either this flight or the next. All of a sudden we would drop quite a ways. They called it hittin' turbulence or an air pocket. It was like drivin' a car over a log pile except there was no ground on the other side of the logs. It sure had me scared and wishin' I were able to pull one of my feed sack quilts over my head. No one else seemed to be bothered. But before long, even that became like a walk in the park as we moved from city to city.

We moved to Kansas City, Missouri, on Thursday, September 5, and went on KOAM-TV where we played on live TV. On Friday, we were still in Kansas City with appearances on KBEY-FM and KBEA-AM radio at Mission, Kansas. The next week, our flight took us into Cincinnati, Ohio, where on September 10, I made my first appearance with two Grammy © winnin' entertainers who would be elected to the Country Music Hall of Fame in 2001. I was sittin' on a bench behind the curtain waitin' my time as I listened to Homer and Jethro perform. I couldn't help myself; I just had to peek out from behind the curtain to see them in their brown jackets as they sang. Homer and Jethro were Henry D. Haynes (1920–1971) and Kenneth C. Burns (1920–1989).

Our appearance was live on WLWT-TV Channel 5 on the "Bob Braun Show." Bob talked to Homer and Jethro, then called me out, and I talked a little about fiddle makin'. Then Bob said, "We see how you make them. Now, let's see how you play them." We hadn't rehearsed or anythin', and I was nowhere near standard key. When I hit "Eighth of January," Homer and Jethro just laid right in behind me without missin' a lick. When everythin' was said and done, I found out they were playin' in B flat for my D. They found the right chord without any effort. We got live calls, and people were sayin' it was the best show Bob Braun ever put on. That was my only appearance with Homer and Jethro, but they were sure good musicians. I would have loved to play in a jam session with them. Passing me as we headed for the studio door after the show, Jethro remarked, "That was great."

We moved along that afternoon on into Detroit, Michigan, where we appeared September 11, on WXYZ -TV (ABC). There, we were on "The Morning Show" with host Bob Hynes. Pete Herschend showed our work and included a talk about my fiddle, so I didn't actually appear on this show.

Next, while in Detroit, I found myself cuttin' up with a clown again as we appeared on WWJ-TV on the "Oopsy Daisy Show." Bob McNea created Oopsy Daisy. He had been Bozo the Clown in Detroit for several years; but, the year before we were there, the station chose not to renew Bozo, and Bob started his own show with his clown Oopsy. A cast of puppets that made his show a bigger favorite with the audience surrounded him.

That afternoon I had my very first shot at becomin' a high fashion model — at least in Silver Dollar City high fashion — sportin' my old fashioned black check dress and bonnet. Don had the unique idea to stand me in the middle of a Detroit street while the wind was whippin' by, givin' me a chill as the Detroit newspaper took my photo. I never understood what the purpose of standin' me in the street was; I guess maybe the comparison of the dress up against the city buildin's behind me.

We headed for Casey Airport to meet Mary Herschend, and then we flew on to Cleveland. That flight took us over Lake Erie and when we reached dry land the farms below looked like a color picture all built in squares. This was one of the worst flights that I remember and not because of the plane or the area. I guess I had developed a sinus infection, so my forehead was bustin'. I even reached up to see if my forehead was bleedin'. When we got ready to land they kind of made a circle. It felt like one side of the plane was lower as we made the turns. To me, it seemed like the plane was flyin' lost. The doctor told me later my sinuses caused my head to hurt.

The week of September 16, Shad Heller, Pete Herschend, Ted Bridges, and I flew to Saint Joseph, Missouri. I remember lookin' down at the clouds, and they looked like pillows of snow. After a week in Missouri, Iowa, and Illinois, we went home before heading to Oklahoma.

We appeared live on "Danny's Day" with Danny Williams on WKY-TV Channel 3 in Oklahoma City at 12:30 p.m. Danny was the announcer on the wrestlin' show that Adren watched sometimes. While there I met

Publicity Tour Itinerary
Week of September 1968

September 16

Saint Joseph, Missouri

"Grace Crawford Show" on KFFQ, newspaper, KUSN radio

Unique: "I saw the original Pony Express stables and two old homes at the site."

Des Moines, Iowa

WHO

Ames, Iowa

WOI-TV Channel 5 taped appearance with Drocus Wheatley at 2:30 p.m.

September 18

Chicago, Illinois

Radio, WMAQ-TV — "Today in Chicago" with Bob Hale (NBC). Pianist Linda Noyle also appeared on the show.

Unique: "Very wet week — We huddled under umbrellas and shook off raincoats to keep from leavin' trails of water behind us."

September 19

Chicago, Illinois

WGN-TV "Top O' the Morning" with the legendary Radio Hall of Fame member Orion Samuelson at 7 a.m. The show included organist Harold Turner.

WGN-TV "The Jim Conway Morning Show"

Unique: "Among the other people appearin' on "The Jim Conway Morning Show" was someone showin' furs and a man that went to the North Pole."

Peoria, Illinois

WMBD Radio in Nixon with Orin Jefferson at 2 p.m.

Unique: "Our group toured the Caterpillar plant."

September 20

Peoria Journal Star, WEEK-TV - "Tom Collins Show"

Shad Heller appeared on "Dorman Keith Show" in Peoria

Springfield, Illinois

Newspaper, WICS Channel 20 with anchors Wayne Cox and Dale Coleman.

Unique: "I visited Lincoln's Tomb in Oak Ridge Cemetery."

Flew home

September 23

Drove to Tulsa and spent a night in Camelot Inn before heading to Oklahoma City.

Carl Tangner, who was a wrestlin' referee. He was a big strong man with muscles but he looked small beside the wrestlers on the TV. After the show, we went to the Oklahoma Publishing Co. but weren't able to get any coverage there.

Next day came a good interview on KFDI radio in Wichita with Bob Roberts. I played the "Eighth of January." My picture was taken for the Wichita Beacon by Howard Sparks with Phyllis Cook writin' the piece. Then we went on to KARD-TV and did an interview with Jean Clark at 2 p.m. I didn't play on this show, but I had my first-ever introduction to a movie star when I met William Lundigan (1914-1975). Since my exposure to films was limited and we didn't have a TV, film stars were not really a fascination to me. Bill had recently done the movie "The Way West" with Kirk Douglas, and he talked about it with Jean as we all did the show. I understand he had been in the movies since the 1930s. Next we appeared on KAKE-TV in Wichita for the "Big Movie Show" with Henry Harvey. I played and whittled. We appeared on the "Joyce Livingston Show" on KTVH-TV Channel 12 in Wichita on Thursday, September 27, at 9 a.m.

For someone who didn't really know much about the movies and folks that starred in them, it was a pretty good week. On Friday, September 27, I met my second movie star, and this one I understand was a big one, not only in height, but also in his popularity as a star. When I walked in to do "The Ida B. Show" on KOCO-TV in Oklahoma City, Oklahoma, I looked around and thought I had stepped into the old west. Ida B. was standin' at the counter, and next to her was a blue-eyed man towerin' above the counter wearin' a cowboy hat and a light leather jacket. Even I knew him. One of the few times we had went up town to the picture show was when we saw his picture, "Rio Bravo." Most folks knew him for his roles as a cowboy. Folks still have pictures of him hangin' in their homes today. His name: John Wayne (1907-1979).

Also standin' around the studio appearin' on the show with us were movie stars and later members of the Country Music Hall of Fame, the Sons of the Pioneers. They often appeared in western films with John, Roy Rogers, and others. John's latest film was not a western, and as Ida B. turned from her cookin' and household hints, she talked with John about a war picture called "The Green Berets." When I walked on the show to do my thing, John smiled and stepped back to watch. As I passed him, I had to look way up at him. After we finished the interview and as the credits rolled on the screen, John turned to me, reached out his hand, took mine, and said, "Great work you are doin' little lady!" He touched the brim of his hat and walked off into the darkness of the studio as I gathered my fiddle makin's while watchin' the Sons of the Pioneers file out. I still can't believe it today as I think back — that I appeared on television with John Wayne and he watched me do my work. That was really somethin'!

Later on the same station, I also appeared on the "Good Morning Ho Ho" with Ho Ho the Clown with Ed Birchall (1923–1988). Ed was very popular with all the kids. He had a great show that I enjoyed appearin' on. While in Oklahoma City, I saw my first city all under one roof. We visited the Shepherd Mall. Never could have imagined somethin' like that when I was growin' up in Alamo.

Pete Herschend headed to Joplin and Pittsburg on October 1, and then on Thursday, October 3, we went to Dallas, Texas. I had never been to Dallas before, and the place took on a different feelin' to most Americans after the 1963 assassination of President John F. Kennedy. It was the start of a very long day as we went to the Dallas Morning News at 3 a.m. and had our picture made. We went to WFAA-TV Channel 8 to appear at 7 a.m. with Jerry Haynes (1927–2011) on his "Mr. Peppermint" show. Jerry dressed in a red and white striped suit with a straw hat, a matchin' bow tie, and cane. I understand that Jerry was the first TV personality to report the news of the assassination locally after watchin' the motorcade pass and hearin' the shots.

That afternoon we went over to Double Day Broadcasting to a new station — KDTV Channel 39. We spent from 2 to 4 in the afternoon with their staff shootin' film. The sound woman even tried her hand at playin' fiddlesticks with me. Sharon Blair from Leslie, Arkansas, and Phil Allen were the emcees. We drove to Fort Worth on Friday, October 4, to be on WBAP radio at 6 a.m., and then we went into their TV studio and had a good interview with Bob Walsh.

We had a little time before our next interview, so we drove the route that President Kennedy took. I could just imagine the crowds gathered on the sidewalks that were out to see President Kennedy and the First Lady as we passed by the Texas Book Depository with it's Hertz time and temperature sign on top, and as we reached the spot on the road where the bullets hit their mark. Such a waste, to end the life of someone so young who was tryin' to make a difference in the lives of regular folks. The thought of this same thing happenin' again to his brother Robert back in June of '68, as he was politickin' for president, made the sadness I felt even heavier as I looked out the window. After the tour, we went on to KRLD-TV where I did a show with Dave Carrington.

The tour brought a lot of firsts to me in my life. Stayin' in hotels, visitin' places I had never been, seein' things I never imagined. As each evenin' came to a close, I would jot down a few lines in my notepads or dash out a few sentences for Adren and the girls on a hotel postcard and drop it in the mail to let them know what was happenin'. While a lot of my time was spent sellin' Silver Dollar City to folks around the country, eventually we all had to get back to doin' what we were talkin' about by actually meetin' with the folks face to face, showin' them what we did, and makin' their trip to the City worth loadin' the kids and grandma up for and comin' to Branson.

Before our sixteen-day fall season in 1968, I never knew much about stardom. In fact, I didn't even have any notion that anyone would ever pay much mind to me. That year though, I learned somethin' — when folks watch you on TV, hear you on the radio, and see you in the newspaper, to them you are a star because millions of folks know about you. As we traveled from city to city that year, we had found our way into the homes of millions and millions of viewers. I had folks from all around the country that fall stop by and take pictures with me, want to hear me play, and watch me work because of the power of TV.

I wasn't any different. I was just me. But because my image had been cut up, traveled through the air, and brought into their livin' rooms and businesses, people had an idea that I was more than I was. I guess my biggest trial ahead was not to let their thinkin' cloud mine. The next few years would only raise the level of the water in the fishbowl that I now found myself inside. I think I managed to keep my head and most of the rest of me above water.

Violet Hensley (left) performs at the 1969 Silver Dollar City fall festival as fans gather around the Gazebo to listen (below).

Violet Hensley at the Silver Dollar City Root Digging Days in 1969. From left are By Kelly, Manual Wood, Art Galbraith (hidden), Jude Herndon, and Sandra Hensley.

Left: Cliff St. James as Corky at KSD-TV in St. Louis, Missouri

Right: Danny Williams from WKY-TV Oklahoma City, Oklahoma

Blacksmith Shad Heller(left) and log hewer Les Vining (right) judge a log hewing contest betweem lye soap maker "Granny" Ethel Huffman (second from left) and fiddle maker Violet Hensley in 1969. Violet was the victor.
Below: Sandra Hensley and Carol Gillum play in the Silver Dollar City Gazebo in October of 1969. Hay is to insulate from the cold.

Here come the hillbillies

In a year in which Neil Armstrong took one small step for man onto the surface of the moon, I also walked into a world I could have never imagined — the world of television and movies. Was it as monumental as man reachin' the moon? Not in the sense of human history, but for me, it was probably just as alien. The same could be said for the new adventures that came in the form of four actors who over the last seven years had taken the country by storm — Buddy Ebsen, Irene Ryan, Donna Douglas, and Max Baer. The cast of "The Beverly Hillbillies" took up residence at Silver Dollar City to film several of their episodes.

Though my television work was allowin' me to meet some stars from that world, this was a unique opportunity for many from the City to get up close and personal with some folks admired by millions of Americans. Don Richardson called and asked me to come up and visit the City durin' the filmin'. The girls and me rode up there as they were shootin' some scenes. I remember my first time lookin' at Irene Ryan (1902–1973) workin'. I noticed that she took a long time to get the lines the way they wanted them in the scene. It may have been close to ten times tryin'. Not gettin' it didn't faze her though. She did it so many times, and I remembered the line myself for a long time. She would say the lines, and then a stunt person would take her place and jump over the rail fence by the City ice cream store and run over by the gazebo. In her, I saw someone like me — similar in size, dress, full of energy, feisty, and fun. Although she was fourteen years my elder, we seemed to hit it off from the start. In between shots, we walked quite a bit together talkin' about things we liked and didn't like. One of those things was ice cream, so we both had an ice cream cone. As I think about it now, we seemed to have a lot in common. She was good with a shotgun, and so was I. Of course, that was part of her fictional character, and it was part of my reality. I still think of her as "Granny." As I watched her and talked with her that day, I drew from her that patience and professionalism is the underlyin' nature of sharin' one's talents, no matter the stage. That is a lesson I have applied since, as I have faced situations that called for patience.

Before long I found myself lookin' up — straight up, it seemed — at Buddy Ebsen (1908–2003), who played Jed, the patriarch of the Clampett clan. He was all dressed up in his Sunday-go-to-meetin' clothes and had his hair slicked back. Like Granny, he took the time to walk and talk with me about the City. I guess in a way I was struck by his down-home nature. I was not even aware of the immense showbusiness legacy that walked along beside me as we talked about the simple, everyday things of life — family, weather, eatin', and what it was like to work at the City.

We were also introduced to Elly Mae (Donna Douglas), who got on with my girls just like they were classmates. She is such a sweet girl! Nancy Kulp (1921–1991), who played Jane Hathaway, was also there, though we only met in passin'. There are a few people in this world that give the appearance of, "Don't touch me; I am better than you are," but I didn't see a bit of that despite the level of stardom these fine folks had attained. I didn't realize then, but this quality time gave me some things to talk about as we made our publicity tour later in the year. At the time, I didn't know the producers planned on featurin' me playin' fiddle in an episode with Sandy playin' the fiddlesticks. Silver Dollar City had shot some film of Sandy and me that was incorporated into one episode as the family wandered around checkin' out the goin's-on at the Silver Dollar City Fair. I think I got $100 for it.

When the episodes were finished, they sent the film out to the City, and they had a showin' for the crew. I didn't get to attend. In fact, I didn't see the performance until several years later because we didn't have a TV that would get that channel. Sandy didn't see it until Pete Herschend sent her some requested copies around 2010. It ran the first time just after we finished our fall tour on October 8, 1969. Me and my fiddle went coast-to-coast with Granny and all the Hillbillies gang, entertainin' millions.

Violet Hensley walks with Buddy Ebsen "Jed Clampett" from "The Beverly Hillbillies" in May 1969 at Silver Dollar City.

Irene Ryan "Granny Clampett" waves to the camera with Chick Allen in the background in May 1969 at Silver Dollar City.

Sandra Hensley, Donna Douglas "Elly Mae Clampett" and Lewonna Hensley share some time in May 1969 at Silver Dollar City.

Violet Hensley shares some Silver Dollar City ice cream with Irene Ryan "Granny Clampett" in May 1969.

Paul Henning's family visits with Violet Hensley at Silver Dollar City in October 1969. Paul was the creator of "The Beverly Hillbillies." From left, are Carol Alice Henning, Violet, and Paul Anthony Henning.

Violet, Sandra, and Adren Hensley perform at Silver Dollar City in 1968.

While Hollywood came to Silver Dollar City that year, it also found its way to our little Yellville — except this time it wasn't in the form of the friendly hill folk but instead gangsters in the form of academy award-winnin' actress Shelley Winters (1920–2006) and of Robert De Niro. They were there shootin' the movie "Bloody Mama" which told a story about notorious "Ma" Kate Barker and her criminally-oriented boys. Robert played her son, Lloyd. Several of us in the community joined the movie as extras. The girls and I joined in as well on August 13 and 14, and they shot a picnic scene to raise money for the volunteer fire department. There were musicians up on the stage, and some folks dancin' when a couple of Ma's boys — Herman (Don Stroud) and his brother Freddy (Robert Walden) — set out on robbin' the collection. The whole crowd took off runnin' after one of them, who was tryin' to steal some wallets while the other brother got the bucket and started shooting. We must have filmed that run about three times. I do remember the bass player's bass bein' busted up in the movie.

Unlike our hillbillies' appearance, these few feet of film represent a passin' moment in film history with us movin' in rhythm with instruments in hand through the pasture before all the gun shootin' started. It was an interestin' experience though, and I saw first-hand all the work that went into workin' on a film set and added a few more famous actors to the list of folks I met.

Based on my notes of our travels, I started my promotional work for the City early in the year before both of these opportunities, travelin' to St. Louis and appearin' on April 18, 1969 for the "The Charlotte Peters Show" on KTVI Channel 2 on the live noon time show. Charlotte became part of an hour-long noonday show in St. Louis in 1947. She sang, did comedy, and interviewed guests in front of a studio audience. I performed my number with a man who played piano along with me. Miss USA 1968 — Miss Dorothy "DIDI" Anstett of Washington State — was also on the show. She gave me a little turtle made out of a walnut shell and a picture of her.

We went to KSD to appear on the "Pevely Playhouse Party," with the Russ David Band. Russ David played jazz and dance music, and his program ran from 12:15 p.m. to 2 p.m. in the auditorium of the Pevely Dairy buildin'. As we began the fall promotional tour, we went into Springfield where we had rooms at the Hotel Lamplighter. We flew to Dayton, Ohio, with pilots J.B. Fraff and Dave Wooten, and then on to Detroit.

On WWJ -TV (NBC) in Detroit, I joined my friend Oopsy on the

"Oopsy Daisy Show." Shad and I played together again, this time kicking off a rendition of "She'll Be Comin' 'Round the Mountain." Oopsy tried his hand at jumpin' one of Grandpa Doubt's ropes. I began teasin' Oopsy about takin' his sidekick, Squiggly Wiggly Worm, a-fishin'. We made our way over to WJR radio in the large Fisher Building where Shad and I played a duet of "Little Brown Jug" and everyone had fun. Grandpa was on, too, as well as a doctor.

Next we appeared in Cincinnati and Cleveland, Ohio. On WKBF in Cleveland, Ohio, I appeared for the afternoon children's program "Captain Cleveland." John Slowey was a ventriloquist, and his sidekick Clem was the dummy. Clem greeted me with a, "Hello, Violet." It amazed me how that dummy looked right at me. Clem asked me, "Did you make them fiddles?" When I replied, "Yes," he complimented me on my work. It was sort of funny havin' a piece of wood tellin' me how much he liked my carvin' on another piece of wood. Almost made him like a traitor to his own kind. It was sure a funny interview.

When we headed back home for a short weekend break from

Publicity Tour Itinerary
Week of September 1969

Dayton, Ohio
WHIO-TV Channel 7 "The Ted Ryan Show" at 1 p.m.

September 15
"The Bette Rogge Show"
Unique: "They had a Renault car inside the studio. Grandpa Doubt made a rope there, and he and Betty jumped rope. Shad and me played 'Turkey in the Straw' on the saw and fiddle."

September 16
Detroit, Michigan
Grandpa Doubt appeared on WXYZ.
WWJ radio with Bob Beasley also included Shad Heller, and Don Richardson

September 17
Cincinnati, Ohio
WCPO Channel 9 "The Nick Clooney Show" with Nick Clooney; Entertainer Len Mink also played guitar on the show.
Unique: Nick is the brother of Rosemary Clooney and father of George Clooney. Shad and I performed "Buffalo Girls."
Cleveland, Ohio
WEWS-TV "The Captain Penny Show" with Ron Penfound
Unique: Ron was on vacation, so I found myself visitin' with Professor Yul Flunk, portrayed by Jim Breslin. The Cleveland Press, Betty Hughes, and Paul Topplestein were then aimin' their cameras at the three of us.
WKYC with Del Donahoo (1923-2014)
Unique: "Shad and I played "Soldier's Joy" as loud as we could there for an outdoor appearance in a park."

September 22
Little Rock, Arkansas
Arkansas Democrat
KTHV Channel 11 with Bob Hicks and Mary Canal

this tour, it was the most important day for me in years. I was bound for Yellville. In addition to talkin' about the City on all these shows, this year my adopted home was mentioned on every show that we did. In a way, I had become the unofficial ambassador from Yellville.

When I arrived home, a huge amount of work awaited me as we moved into and slept in our new house. My two daughters and the three boys did the movin'. I remember how new the house was and how beautiful the scenery was lookin' out the new windows. I thought to myself how I would-not have to sweep the spider webs down, shoo a mouse or swat a wasp. But it didn't take long until I was doin' all three. Amazin' how they can find their new homes too.

My time there was short. By Sunday I was drivin' again towards Branson to find my seat in the plane headed toward Colorado by way of Wichita, Kansas. As we flew, I passed much of my time lookin' down at the world below. The fields were large and terraced. The houses were miles apart, with only a few cattle grazin' in the green pastures below. I saw no roads or traffic. I remember spyin' only one car on the road

Publicity Tour Itinerary
Week of September 1969

September 23

Milwaukee, Wisconsin

WTMO radio with Carol Cotter

Unique: While in Milwaukee, we visited AAA Insurance and while we visited, I was asked to show my fiddles. I got them out of the car and clowned around a bit playin' the fiddle. While in the office as I did my thing, all the workers stood still to look on. They took photos for the AAA magazine.

September 24

WISN radio with Charlie Hanson

Unique: Shad Heller and John Corbin both played "Cindy" on mouth bows on the show. A mouth bow is a piece of flat wood bent like a bow and arrow with a peg in one end connected to a string tied to the other end. The bow was held against the side of your mouth with the mouth held open at different points to create different sounds from the bow as the player strums the string on the bow. Shad and I did a duet, and Grandpa was given an advertisement to do on gowns for his new wife.

Shad Heller appeared on WISN TV channel 12 for "Dialing for Dollars" with Howard Gernette.

Peoria, Illinois

WMBD Channel 31 (CBS) at 12:30 p.m. "Man on the Street"

Springfield, Ill.

St. Louis, Missouri

September 26

KSD-TV Channel 5

Unique: Shad Heller, John Corbin, and I were taken to a park and we sang and played "In the Evenin' by the Moonlight" as we walked toward and away from the camera in the park.

KDNL Channel 30 with Jack Miller as "Mr. Patches."

as we flew over Colorado. The world looked level as far as I could see. Eventually, the sights transitioned to sagebrush and a few dust bowls, and the world I passed through revealed the cattle livin' there had to go for miles to reach water. When I was not lookin' out the window, I was battlin' my sinuses bringin' out blood.

As we drew our promotional tour to a close, I went back home and prepared for my third fall festival at the City. By now, I found what I was doin' to be as comfortable as puttin' on a pair of house shoes. Of course, I never wore those on TV.

Publicity Tour Itinerary
Week of September 1969

September 29

Denver, Colorado

KBTV Channel 9 with Tony Pepper as Ben Avery

September 30

KOA TV Channel 4 with Merrie Lynn

KLZ radio with Evan Slack

AAA Insurance for pictures inside and outside the buildin'

Colorado Springs, Colorado

KKTV with Bill Bruce

October 1

KRDO radio with Bill Yeager

Unique: "I even called hogs and cows on radio, though none showed up."

Me, Shad, and Leslie Jones got a photo taken by the newspaper out by the Rock Street Bank.

Musicians play on the set of "Bloody Mama" in Yellville, Arkansas, in 1969 including Lonnie Avey, Charlie Richardson, and Bookmiller Shannon.

Left: Russ Scott was Captain Dooley, host of Lunchtime Little Theatre. Right: Russ Scott was also Binky the Clown, host of The Fun Club. Both shows were on KWGN channel 2 in Denver, Colorado.

Jack Miller was Mr. Patches on KDNL channel 30 St Louis, Missouri.

America's stage

Spring rolled around fast in 1970 as my work began again on the road. This time my daughter, Sandy, was on the trip with me. We left from the School of the Ozarks, now called College of the Ozarks, in Point Lookout, Missouri, where Sandy was enrolled and takin' elementary education classes. We stepped onto the Cessna, Sunday, April 19. Our pilot was Dale Moore, and we began a run to Des Moines, Omaha, Lincoln, Kansas City, St. Joseph, back to Kansas City, and then to Denver. We landed at 6:31 p.m. and spent the night in a Holiday Inn.

With each appearance on the tour, it seemed even more people knew about the City and all of us who helped to sing its praises. While I won't bore you further with year after year of these travels, I wanted you to get the feel of our time on the road as we traveled for the City. The visibility I gained through all the TV exposure brought other media into my life and one of the earliest examples was when National Geographic Magazine featured a story by Bruce Dale highlightin' the Ozarks in November 1970. They included a picture of Jimmy Driftwood and interviewed and took a photo of me as well as several of some pet skunks we had. A pair of skunks took up residence with us in 1966 as we were livin' in Yellville in a rental while our house was bein' built. Adren had killed their mother while bush hoggin' and brought them home. They were not de-scented, and, as a result, the kids were sprayed a few times. They sprayed if you surprised them, which was done only by accident. We used tomato juice to get rid of the odor. National Geographic came to our house durin' this time and took lots of pictures of those skunks as well as the fiddle makin' and playin'. We don't know if the skunk pictures were ever used, but I am sure the journalists had some stories to share when they returned home.

Silver Dollar City opened doors for me I could have never imagined. I had been seen nationally on television carryin' on the skills shared with me by my father and the other fiddlers back in Alamo. Now, a new door opened as the Smithsonian would focus its attention on the state of Arkansas and all of those who proudly continued the skills we were taught. There were seventy-three crafters and performers from Arkansas who went in 1970. The Festival of American Folklife put me on the national stage in a different way as we headed for Washington, D.C., for the event held for several days around July 4. I had to make me a toolbox out of plywood and ship it ahead with my hand ax and all the frame

Publicity Tour Itinerary
Week of April 1970

April 19 Flight on Cessna with pilot Dale Moore Destinations: Des Moines, Omaha, Lincoln, Kansas City, St. Joseph, back to Kansas City, and then to Denver.

April 20

Des Moines, Iowa

WHO radio with Lee Kline also Sandy Hensley and Shad Heller

WHO-TV Channel 13 with Don Warren and Floppy the Dog (Duane Ellett) at noon. KRNT-TV and taped a show at 1:45 p.m.

Unique: "Sandy picked the guitar while I whittled, and then we played with fiddlesticks. We ate at the Hyatt House Hotel."

Des Moines Register and Tribune newspapers on 8th and Locust streets included an interview and picture of Sandy and I with fiddlesticks.

April 21

Omaha, Nebraska

WOW Channel 6

Unique: "Shad plugged the upcomin' Beverly Hillbillies episodes, though he got his stations mixed up because we weren't on a CBS station."

KMTV Channel 3

Unique: "Chick Allen, Shad Heller, and us played 'She'll Be Comin' Round the Mountain.' Sandy and I played 'Take Me Back to Tulsa.'"

KETV Channel 7 with Joni Ballion at 2:30 p.m.

Unique: "This was an especially fun show for all of us. We all played, and Chick danced afterwards with George Murphy and the crew. While there, a lady named Dee DeWright, a violinist who had written letters to me through a magazine article in 'Workbench,' came and got me and took me out to her house not far from the TV station for a visit. When I got back to the station, we all went and grabbed some roast beef sandwiches at Brander's Drugs in Omaha."

works and the woods I was gonna work on. The crafters were off in a big park-like thing (the National Mall) with an awnin' over each one for a tent and ropes around each for a wall. Durin' the day, we would work at our makin's as folks visited with us. People asked me a lot of questions. It was sort of like what I did at Silver Dollar City each year except there were a lot more people at one time. We had a blacksmith, a chair maker in Jack McKutchin, one person grindin' corn, one makin' apple head and corncob head dolls, and others. Junior Cobb was the wood carver, but I was the only instrument maker.

Jimmy Driftwood took care of the musicians. He had brought several performers who appeared regularly at Mountain View. There were four black girls called the Loving Sisters from Little Rock, Arkansas. From other states were Mother Maybelle Carter and the Carter Family, and Ralph Stanley, who was still continuin' the sounds of the Stanley Brothers. We would do shows in the evenin' after a full day of showin' our crafts. I was excited bein' around some of the musicians I had heard on record. This gave me the chance to spend some quality time with Maybelle Carter. I talked a lot with Maybelle and Anita Carter and had a chance to discuss the Carter Family tunes I remember learnin' like Cyclone of Rye Cove, Maple on the Hill, Weepin' Willow Tree, and Rosewood Casket.

We performed on the stage of the Sylvan Theater at the Washington Monument. There was a platform stage with lots of mikes in front of us. I had never seen so many people in my life as when I walked out on the stage. They told me there were 50,000. There were even folks sittin' on the amplifiers. From my vantagepoint, people looked small. Grown folks appeared like children because they were so far away. I was a little bit nervous but not too bad. I thought I liked the bigger crowd. Once you got started entertainin', the more people the better you felt.

Jimmy Driftwood emceed bringin' on the different performers, and each group would have three songs each night. Among the Mountain View folks were Olan and Retha Finley. He did a dance, and Retha clapped her hands as Sandy and I backed them on our instruments. Bookmiller Shannon played the banjo with Lonnie Avey playin' guitar. Lonnie Lee also played guitar. Almeda Riddle sang acapella, and Ollie Gilbert told jokes. She would get to tell her joke, and she wanted to tell another one. On our show, Sandy played guitar, I played fiddle, and Bob Blair played the banjo. When we finished up, they would get the whole, entire group on stage, and we would all do a feature and play together. I remember one time Curly Ray Cline played Eighth of January differently from me. He couldn't go over each part of it twice, so I played, and he faked it. But we took turn about, since I couldn't play Arkansas Traveler — he played and I faked it.

On one of the days, I wandered by and noticed a black guitar player leanin' up agin a tree. I had my fiddle in hand so I went over and we sawed off a few tunes — Soldier's Joy, Liberty, and Eighth of January. I didn't know until later that he was Mance Lipscomb, the famous blues player.

I had traveled a lot the last few years, and I knew that things were a little different in the big cities than they were back home in Arkansas and Missouri. The young men were wearin' their hair longer, the men and women had clothes that made them look different from regular folks. They called them hippies. There were lots of them there. It was just a few months before when over a half million people had protested the Vietnam War in the same area where we were now performin'. Organizers were concerned about our safety, that some protesters might decide the festival was a place to make a point. They were right. Some folks couldn't let it pass, and they had boys breakin' car windows with pop bottles, and they had to get tear gas after them. The police hurried all of us away to safety, so all I saw was the risin' smoke of the tear gas as they tried to get them under control. Our show the night of the protest was moved inside a nearby buildin'. It probably took two hours to get all the entertainers through. When we arrived inside, Doc Watson and Merle Watson were on stage with Lisa Watson. Doc said that was Lisa's first appearance on stage.

I can't say whether America should have been at war. I always thought those things were decided by men that knew much more about it than I did. I worried that Russell, who was in the Army, or Frog, who was in the Navy, might have to go over to fight. In fact, that fall, Eddie was drafted but never had to go to war. The sadness of it all was that so many mothers like me had sons go off to serve, and many did not come back home. If their deaths are to have meanin', then the war must be somethin' just.

When a
National Geographic
photographer came to
document
Violet Hensley's fiddle
making, they were also
fascinated by
pet skunks that
Lewonna Hensley plays
with in this photo.

Fiddlin' in a Basket
A Photography Class
project by
Lewonna Hensley.

The Silver Dollar City gang take off from the airport in Denver, Colorado, on April 24, 1970. From left are Dale Moore, pilot; Violet Hensley; Shad Heller; Sandra Hensley; and Chick Allen.

Violet Hensley and Sandra Hensley pose in front of KETV in Omaha, Nebraska, on April 21, 1970.

Silver Dollar City folks Shad Heller, Sandra Hensley, Violet Hensley, and Chick Allen appear on WGIN in Lincoln, Nebraska, in 1970.

Violet and the Hensleys entertain at Silver Dollar City.

Mother Maybelle Carter (center) performs with members
of the Carter Family in July of 1970 in Washington D.C.

Left: Sandra and Violet Hensley give a little dance inside the Museum of Natural History in Washington D.C. in 1970 after being safely moved away from tear gas at the Festival of American Folklife.
Below: Checking in at event are (from left) Sandra Hensley, Violet Hensley, Junior Cobb (back), Jimmy Nelson, Betty Copeland, and Mac McCormick.

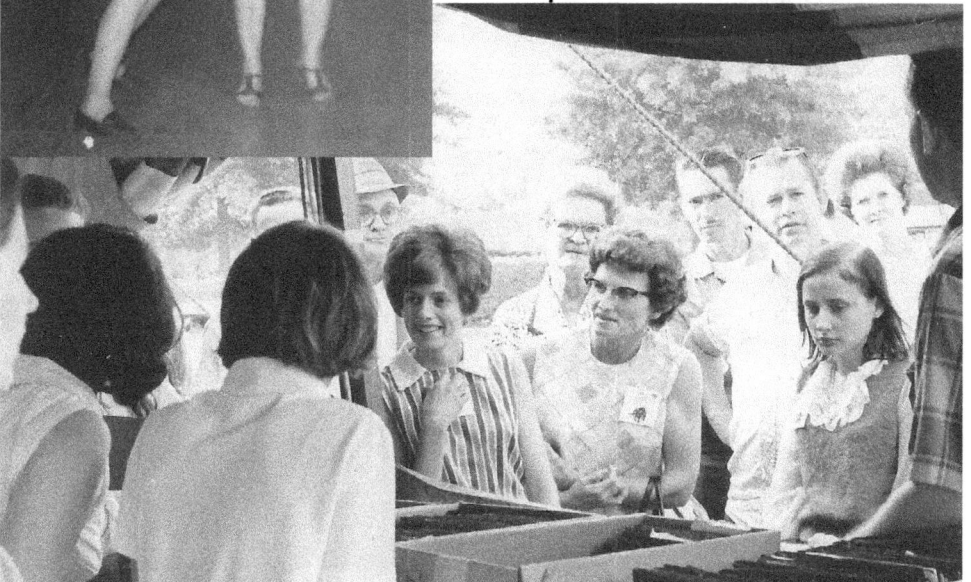

Violet Hensley visits with Gladys McFadden and the Loving Sisters on Sunday, July 5, 1970 in Washington, D.C.

A crowd watches Violet as she plays with the support of a passerby in her Festival of American Folklife booth in 1970 in Washington, D.C.

Californy and America's Storytellers

Just like the Clampetts, I was headed to Beverly Hills — well, at least to Hollywood to make another national TV appearance — in July 1970. Shad Heller and I flew out there and, to make us feel at home, Paul Henning (1911–2005), the creator of "The Beverly Hillbillies," met us and Don Richardson at the airport. He took us to the hotel, and then we went on over to NBC to do our appearance with the already-legendary personality Art Linkletter (1912–2010) on his show, "Life with Linkletter." Art was the interviewer askin' me questions about fiddle makin', and then I did a little fiddle playin'. Shad played the hand saw with me before talkin' about the blacksmith shop.

I met another big film star — Clint Eastwood — doin' this show who had out a new movie called "Two Mules for Sister Sara." It wasn't like meetin' John Wayne, but Clint was just as tall when I looked up into his strong eyes. Though he was supposed to be a tough guy, he had a pleasantness about him that came through as we spoke. He seemed to enjoy watchin' us as we did our part with Art. While I didn't see his movies, Adren was a big fan of his TV show,"Rawhide," from years before, and I had watched a few of those episodes and knew his name. That evenin', they presented Clint with a rifle, and I got a clock radio — a four-by-eight sized thing. It didn't last too many years. I hope Clint can still shoot his rifle!

After the show, Paul took us out to his house. He and his wife Ruth lived in a big mansion. I remember that he had built a cut-out area in one of the corners of the house. It was enclosed with glass. I told him I would sit right there and make fiddles all the time if I lived there. We went all through the house and talked. He gave me a couple of books on old-fashioned clothin'. We headed back to the hotel, and Paul came and picked us up later and took us to dinner where Elly Mae, Jed, and Granny (Donna Douglas, Buddy Ebsen, and Irene Ryan) joined us. I remember Elly Mae most of all because she had just washed her hair and had it up in a stockin' cap. We had a nice visit that evenin'.

It is amazin' the path that I was walkin' on. What a long ways from Alamo. But no matter how far one travels and how great the experience, eventually the road leads back home — and sometimes within the walls of home, the clock will toll and the times will try a woman's soul. No matter how much success one has in life beyond the walls of home, it is only to make the time and the loved ones livin' within those walls have the opportunity for better times. My national success did not make our little family immune to heartache and sickness. My son Frog (Gary) went in the Navy in 1969. He was stationed in Memphis. On November 23, 1970, there was a knock at the door that brought me to answer it. An Army man from Bruno was standin' there. I was by myself since Adren was workin' at Flippin doin' brickwork. The man said to me, "Your son got hurt." I asked, "Is he hurt bad?" His reply still rings in my ears so many years later, "I'm afraid so. I'm afraid he is dead." He took me up to where Adren was. I came back with him, and we sat around as sad as we could be. Wonnie was in school at Yellville-Summit. She got home soon after Adren and I did and started the phone calls to other family members.

My son was datin' a girl named Mary; they apparently were havin' an argument. She didn't want to go home, but she got out of the car near Senatobia, Mississippi, and started walkin'. She told me later, "He waited there a little bit and took off." Her mother had told him to be careful when he picked her up. Up the road a ways he ran out of gas and left the car in the median and began walkin' towards Memphis. It was fifteen degrees, and he had his coat over his head. It was a seventy-mile-per-hour zone. Evidently, he heard a car and was goin' to other side of road to get out of the way. The driver said later, he saw him crossin' and tried to miss him and they both chose to dodge in the same direction. Unfortunately, they met rather than missin'.

I thought my world had ended. I didn't think I would ever go back to

Silver Dollar City. Adren sold his car for $900, and the military insurance was $17,000. I would have given every dime I had to have Gary back, but that was not to be. After much thought, I knew he would want me to go on, so I used the money to pay off the house, makin' us free and clear of debt. My mind wasn't free though. I could hardly stand it. You can't understand until it happens to you. Then you can feel what another goes through when they lose a child. Gary wouldn't have wanted me to quit. He was proud of me bein' at the City, so I did return.

Adren, the girls, and me found a new normal as we carried on with day-to-day livin', but before we could turn around good, we were addin' to our family. Adren and me had a large family, but there was always room for others at our table. Our children's friends would often stay with us briefly. One friend who came to stay two or three days became part of our family, doin' what the other kids did, sharin' chores, and helpin' us in every way imaginable. In February '71 as a sophomore in high school, Wilma Plant became a foster daughter to Adren and me. She went where the family went and did what we did.

She didn't play an instrument but would sometimes join in with the jawbone if Wonnie wasn't playin' it. She was ever eager to help and to please, and she was ready to load and unload the car, run errands, and do anything that needed to be done. Even after goin' on to college and makin' a life of her own, forty-one years later she is still a foster daughter who never misses a family gatherin' and always does her part to share in family projects. She married Sandra's brother-in-law, Doug Flagg. They even added one to the number of my grandchildren — LeighAnna Flagg Schesser. She and her husband, Jacob Benedict Schesser added another great grandchild, Benedict Jacob Schesser.

As we learned to move forward, we found life was full of unexpected gifts. Adren and I was at home one evenin' when I got a call from a news person wantin' to know if I would be home the next day. I told them I would be workin' at the Yellville Hospital, but they could come and I would see them after work. I had been workin' at the hospital for a while. I worked in housekeepin'. As I cleaned the bedside tables, bathrooms, and food table, I talked to the patients and often sang to them. A man came to the door at home the next day and said, "I am Charles Kuralt. I was told in Washington that while I was in Arkansas, I needed to see the Whittlin' Fiddler of Yellville." Charles (1934–1997) asked me if this was the right place. I invited him to come on in, and he said he would like to do some filmin'. He asked where to hook this and that. Sandy and Wonnie were in college at the time, and we were just fixin' to go up to get them and go to Hot Springs to visit my oldest daughter. He said he thought it would be worth my while to wait over a day.

The crew lived in a Winnebago and spent a couple of days parked down below the house. They set lights up in each corner of the west end of my kitchen. I went on to work and left them there. Adren helped them with anything they needed, and I came in at night about four o'clock, and we just visited. On Saturday mornin' we did tapin' and it took quite a while. Sandy came in from college, so I had Sandy here to play the guitar with me on the show. One thing that I didn't realize they were gonna do at the time that surprised me later had to do with my feet. I said to Charles, "Let me get my shoes on." I was barefooted. He said, "We won't bother your feet." I thought it was kind of funny and figured my feet would be out of the picture. But when it came out, there I am stompin' my right bare foot. Charles sat beside me in the kitchen doin' the interview, and one of the main comments I remember was, "I see you play good and make them good. Which do you like best?" I replied, "If I'm playin', I don't want to quit, and if I'm whittlin', I don't want to quit."

I played "Soldier's Joy," "Eighth of January," and "Buffalo Nickel." They stayed around through the rest of the day takin' down all they had set up, and then they went on their way — but not without a little more help from Adren. It had rained good, and our street was dirt back then. In order to get the Winnebago up the hill, Adren had to hook our van up to the Winnebago and pull them out.

I really liked Charles. He had an interestin' personality. The interview aired in February of 1973 in his feature "On the Road with Charles Kuralt." I had to go to a neighbor's house to see it 'cause I didn't have a television. Needless to say, while I was enthused by the program, my, it really tickled me to see my bare feet tappin' out the time. Up until this point in my life, I had almost kept my home life and my celebrity life in two neat little boxes of their own. With this interview, things really changed. The exposure brought even greater reaction than I could have imagined as we received visitors from around the country almost everyday in our home for a long time after it aired. We also got calls and letters wantin' to buy one of my fiddles. One man even traveled to our house from Pennsylvania to buy a fiddle. My stage had moved from TV stations, stages, and Silver Dollar City to my livin' room. Now the home box was unwrapped for everyone to see — bare feet and all.

The next year our home would be rocked with illness as an ear, nose, and throat doctor in Harrison, Arkansas, discovered in May 1974 that Adren had cancer. He always called me "Mama." He said, "Mama, I'm stayin' hoarse too long." He burned some cedar down in the basement, but he found out it was not the cedar burnin' that caused the problem. They told him smokin' was the cause of it. I was worried about him smokin' in the first place. By now Adren had quit drinkin'. His last drunk was Christmas 1973, but he still smoked. Once they told him about the cancer, he threw the cigarettes away and never took another one after that. He seemed to take it calmly, so it helped me not to be so worried. I wouldn't tell him I was worried about it. He went then to the VA Hospital in Little Rock, and they scraped his throat and told him not to say a word for ten days. He went back, and they scraped it a second time and finally got it all. He didn't have to take chemotherapy or anything.

A lot of couples don't get along. For us, everything changed for the better because Adren quit drinkin' and smokin', and it got better on me. We never did word fight. He might come in and say somethin' that he wouldn't say sober. He might come in at midnight and want somethin' to eat, and I would fix it. We still got along. After the experience, he went back to doin' work with black toppin'. He told me sometimes he would catch himself reachin' in his shirt pocket for a cigarette. This cancer thing was so scary to me then; I was afraid to lose Adren. I could have never seen what was in store though. This experience changed him. A change that started when he quit drinkin' came into bloom after the cancer. He lived twenty-four more years. Those were some of our best years. We did more together, more visitin' with each other and with others, and we played more music. In a way, I found the man that I was really lookin' for when I first looked into his brown eyes on that path when I was just a girl. The endless stretches of uncertainty due to his drinkin'; the unantici- pated moves from one place to another; tryin' to make ends meet in the middle without a rope long enough to tie — these had all passed on, and these happier times were what all of those trials led me to. It was worth it.

Art Linkletter watches as Violet Hensley
fiddles and Shad Heller plays the saw.

Violet Hensley performs at
Silver Dollar City in 1974.

"The Beverly Hillbillies" — Buddy Ebsen, Max Baer Jr.,
Donna Douglas, and Irene Ryan ride in the truck.
Violet shared some time with them during her visit to Hollywood.

Charles Kuralt watches Violet Hensley fiddle in her kitchen for a 1970s
appearance on the CBS Evening News.

The Hensley family gathers at Gary Hensley's funeral. From left are Lewonna, Sandra, Eddie, R.G., Russell, Calvin, Marvin, Beatrice, Violet and Adren.

Above: Gary Hensley

Left: From left are, Wilma Plant, Sandra Hensley, and Lewonna Hensley.

Violet Hensley works on fiddle number eight in the Gazebo at Silver Dollar City in 1971. She gave this fiddle to her son Calvin.

Adren and Violet Hensley with the cat Sunyatse in Yellville in 1970.

Both Violet Hensley and Adren Hensley enjoyed competing in the cross-saw contest at Silver Dollar City. Left: Violet poses with her partner when she won in 1970. Below: Adren Hensley competes in 1980.

Jimmy Driftwood and Captain Kangaroo

Jimmy Driftwood (1907–1998) would come back into my performance life in 1977 and 1978 as he invited me to join a couple of tours he
hosted. He liked to take me since I was a woman makin' fiddles and I
play. By this time Jimmy had become the champion of Arkansas's musical traditions around the world. His work at the height of his stardom in
the early 1960s won him numerous Grammys ®. I thought Jimmy was a
wonderful, honest and carin' person. He didn't think he was better than
anybody else. He and his wife Cleda got along nicely. He had a farm and
ran some cattle. They always told me "You are welcome to come in my
home. My home is your home."

On these tours, we went to different colleges and universities in
Aurora, Mo., Kansas, Torrington, Wyo., Valparaiso, Ind., and Coldwater,
Mich. And on one of the trips we went to Chicago. We would set up in
the auditorium and show crafts, like doll and basket makin'. I didn't do
any showin' in fiddle makin' on these trips. They would have a little stage
we played music on.

While many played both tours there were some changes from year to
year. Among those workin' with us were Mike Sutter (guitar and vocals),
Lonnie Avey (guitar), Bookmiller Shannon (banjo), Cathy Barton (banjo
and hammered dulcimer), Glen Branscum (guitar and vocals), Marilyn
Horsley (singer) Olan and Retha Finley (dancing). Lonnie Lee and Jimmy

Driftwood drove the vans carryin' us all.

Jimmy would sing a song, maybe one or two and then we would do our share. Once he told Cathy Barton that I had the habit of movin' around away from the mike. He told Cathy to tell me not to swing so much at one of our shows.

One of my greatest honors in life as a fiddle maker was when Jimmy bought my number 14 fiddle to take to Washington, D.C. to give to U.S. Sen. Robert Byrd (1917-2010) of West Virginia. He was a fiddler himself that brought a lot of attention to our music by his position in Washington.

The last time I saw Jimmy and Cleda, she helped Jimmy up on stage and she also assisted him in rememberin' the words to his next verse in the songs. After he passed away, they did a tribute for him down at Mountain View and I went down and played on that. In many ways Jimmy Driftwood opened the ears of America to the traditional sounds of mountain music with his unique songs sharin' history and music in a way that uplifted the listener. He almost reached in and grabbed the kid within us with his words and made us want to listen.

If you win the hearts of the children, it is amazin' how they can be drawn to the crafts and music we were makin'. After years of local TV, I think I had been on camera with every clown or puppeteer that entertained the youth of America. At least it seemed that way. Even though I didn't wear makeup, sometimes, I just look in the mirror before goin' on to make sure one of those big red noses has not accidentally migrated to my face.

This year I would get on the biggest children's stage of the last 15 years, Captain Kangaroo. Captain Kangaroo was a character portrayed by Bob Keeshan (1927–2004) that ran every mornin' on the CBS network. It was September when we went to New York City. We landed in Teterboro, NJ and drove under the Hudson River to our New York motel. We arrived there early and prepared for the show. I didn't see Bob until we came on the set. He was very friendly, what I call common sense people.

While he would introduce the segment that featured several of us from the City, we had Judy Graham who made dolls, Ethel Huffman who made lye soap, and another man that did blacksmithin', possibly Shad Heller. I actually interacted on the show with Mr. Green Jeans (Hugh "Lumpy" Brannum, 1910–1987). I played for him a little bit and got a lot of cheers and handclappin' from the little studio audience. I also danced with Mr. Green Jeans, so they must have played a little music for us for rhythm. Captain Kangaroo praised my playin' as we finished the segment.

My schoolteacher had said to me as a child, I should be a teacher or run a nursery. In a way the opportunities that fiddle makin' and playin' allowed me, made me a teacher, and with it I reached more children than I ever would have in a one-room schoolhouse. I had stood side by side with television's entertainin' children educators that with a bit a laughter and some fun taught a generation of Americans about the world around them. I came into many of their TV studio classrooms each year and taught another class of kids as they watched. I shared what my dad and other fiddlers had taught me. Did any of them become a fiddle maker or a fiddler because of it? It is possible but only they know the impact it had on their lives. I can only hope I was able to improve their understandin' and appreciation for what I loved to do, and maybe simply by them seein' my enthusiasm, they were able to use that same type of energy in what ever they did.

Violet got this view of travel with Jimmy and Cleda Driftwood on a 1977 tour.

Violet shares her skills with children across the country on the CBS children's program "Captain Kangaroo" with "Mr. Green Jeans" (Hugh "Lumpy" Brannum).

Jimmy Driftwood presents one of Violet's creations to
Sen. Robert Byrd in Washington, D.C.
Below: Violet Hensley and Curly Haworth perform at the
Wagonworks Barn at Silver Dollar City in 1979.

Sassy sixties

I have heard folks ask, "What was the best time of your life?" Well that's easy, the best time is today. You might think it'd be your twenties, thirties, forties, etc. They are all good. They just take a different shape and include different things.

All my children were on their own by the 1980s, and it was just Adren and me enjoyin' ourselves. We were in our sixties, playin' music and doin' craft shows like the Forsyth Arts and Crafts Festival in Forsyth, Missouri. I did that one for 20 years (1972–1992). We had an old school bus made into a camper that we would travel in which was perfect for three-day events like Forsyth. The only drawbacks were that the festival was in August when it was so hot. Even though there was a good crowd on Saturday, we didn't make enough to pay to go there. I paid to set up the first year just like the other crafters, but after that they wanted me to come, so I would go without a fee. I took the fiddles and sold my little characters I carved — horses, geese, dogs, and little pins — turtles, ducks, rabbits, butterflies, and squirrels, and two designs of cats and rabbits. We still did our work each year for Silver Dollar City as well. That was as much a part of us now as breathin'.

As I said earlier, our home was always open, and that was even truer when it came to my grandchildren. Our son Russell had to go serve in Korea in December of 1979, so I kept his sons, Michael, who was twelve, and Chris, who was five. I kept them for about a year and a half. They helped me with the garden, and Mike played the jawbone when Adren and I performed. Havin' the boys around helped us stay connected with young people, and I thought it was important to share what I did with children.

Through the years, I went to several schools showin' what I did to children of all ages. Sandy was usually with me providin' the rhythm and playin' the specialty instruments. The kids were usually in the fourth or fifth grades, but sometimes they were of all ages, and teachers would bring several classes into one room where we performed. I would open up by sayin', "Well, I know one thing every child in this room looks for'ed to doin'." Maybe one would speak up and say, "Play the fiddle." They could not ever guess what I had in mind, so I would add, "Somethin' you're all lookin' for'ed to gettin' old enough to do." I would pause and let the anticipation build and then say, "You are lookin' for'ed to gettin' old enough to drive a car." That would usually bring a laugh out of them. Then I would tell them about makin' fiddles. First, I would show them the pieces of wood and how I bent the sides. Then I would show them how to whittle a little, to shape the back and front. Then they would get anxious and want to hear it played. We would play a few tunes. I would start off with, "She'll Be Comin' 'Round the Mountain" and put the fiddle on top of my head while playin' it. When I started performin' at schools, I would let a couple of students come up and play. We had little clackers, with two pieces of board that bumped against the centerpiece, and maracas, two sets of spoons, a Terrapin shell, and a jawbone. I soon realized that was a mistake because all the children wanted to get up, so then I would get the teachers to do it. Then the kids would love that too. I couldn't give them all the chance to play spoons or play the jawbone. We just didn't have the time. But in most places they would all get a chance to walk by and look at all the fiddle makin's and the instruments before they went back to their rooms. After I was through, the kids would be so gracious. They would always want to come up and give me a big hug.

Youth, however, came in all sizes all the way up to those college kids, and I wanted to make sure I didn't miss a one when the opportunity arose. We got a chance to perform down in Mississippi at the junior college at Senatobia in early April 1974. Adren, Sandy, Wonnie, me, and our little black dog, Happy, went down. When we got there, I asked about a motel room and a place to dog sit. We wound up stayin' in the dorm as we entertained a couple of days, and the college kids sat with Happy.

From there, we went to another event called the Sycamore Fair near Nashville, Mississippi. There was a fiddler's contest, and they had a square dancin' competition. I entered in the fiddle contest, but I never could relax and just play like I should when competin'. So I didn't win. There were three dancers that needed another partner to enter the square dancin' competition, so Sandy joined in. She had never danced in public before. She happened to be wearin' the same color shirt and slacks as her partner — pink and burgundy. The other couple had not danced together either, and their shirt and slacks were the same color, blue. They tied for second place. In the dance-off, Sandy's group won.

While there, either a radio or TV crew interviewed Wonnie. They asked her what instrument she was playin', and she said, "a Jackass-a-phone." They got all excited and said, "You can't say that on the air!" She said that because that's what Chick Allen from the Baldknobbers called it. She learned to play it from watchin' him, only he played a mule's jaw-bone and she played a Shetland pony's jawbone. When the interviewer asked if it was hard to tune, she said "no" and pulled on some loose teeth. Then she said she couldn't play in B flat because B flat was missin', and she pointed to where a tooth was missin'. There was a patient where I worked in the hospital who was admitted because his horse had reared up and gone over back'ards on top of him. I told him about Wonnie playin' on Chick Allen's jawbone, and when the patient went home he found the horse had killed a pony. Later, he brought the jawbone to us.

Of course, I was still amazed with each passin' year at the number of opportunities I received to share my carvin' and music. Though fiddle makin' was my entrance into notoriety, as time passed, I was called upon to share other aspects of my experiences for TV and articles. One of those times was when Arkansas Educational Television visited me for a pro-gram on July 18, 1982 to discuss the art of preservin' natural herbs. They came to the house and had me dryin' sage in the oven on very low heat. We had purslane. You melt it down like spinach, or you can chop it into salad. A dishpan of purslane will disappear to a teacup full.

When I was seventy years old, Don Richardson thought he would try to get me on the Johnny Carson show, so he set up a three-way call at the City so I could speak with the lady talent booker on the show. The con-versation was rather short, but as Don Richardson remarked to her, I had "a thing about bein' truthful." I didn't realize it at the time, but I later decided I didn't say the right thing at one point in the interview when she asked me, "What is the greatest thing you would like to do?" I guess the answer should have been appearin' on the Johnny Carson show, but it wasn't. I said, "Play my fiddle on the Grand Ole Opry." So then, she told Don, "I don't think she would be funny enough for the show." So that was that.

Beginning in the late '80s, for about a year, we went every Saturday night to perform live on KCTT radio with host John Adams in Yellville. Adren and on occasion Sandy and my granddaughter Amanda Flagg would join me. We made intermittent appearances on the show after that until 1992.

One day in 1987, in answer to a knock at the door, I found a Japanese girl, Marika Sonja, all the way from Tokyo. I don't know how she found me. She and her crew wanted to do an interview for what they described as "Tokyo's 60 Minutes." The tape I received of the show included the words "World Network" on the set. They took a variety of shots for the program includin' the horse in the pasture. They rung the wind chimes by the door and shot me as I told her to come in. Inside, she focused on the rattles in the sound hole of my fiddle. It turned out she was a violinist, so we did some playin' together on a tune she made up sort of like "Boil Them Cabbage Down." We were goin' to Silver Dollar City, so they came along and took a bunch of shots of Adren pullin' the camper in at the campground. He sort of got aggravated because he had it ready to hook up and they wanted him to drive it in again.

The next day, she came to see us in the City. I said, "Here's Sonya Marika," mixin' her name up, but she came up on the platform and we played together again. She followed me on "Going up Brushy Fork." The next day, before they left, she came back and handed me a long envelope. Inside of it there was a hundred dollars apiece for Adren and me. Adren felt better then. They later sent me a video of the show. I always wanted to know what I sounded like in Japanese... and you know, I didn't sound any different.

Left: Violet Hensley, Adren Hensley and their grandson Chris perform at the Silver Dollar City Fall Festival.

Below: Violet Hensley's wood carvings

Violet Hensley performing in California. From left are Adren, Lewonna (Hensley) Nelson, Violet, and Jay Round of Grandview, Michigan.

Violet Hensley drys herbs in her kitchen.

Violet Hensley performs with Lewonna, Sandra and Adren on April 5, 1974 at Northwest University in Senatoba, Mississippi.

Violet Hensley, Adren Hensley, Sandra Flagg and Greg Patrick (hidden) jam in 1981. Violet is playing fiddle number twenty-six.

Sandra (Hensley) Flagg and Violet Hensley

A long goodbye

A heavy fog began settlin' over our good times as Alzheimer's began to cloud Adren's mind. We still played some, and it didn't seem that the effects bothered his guitar playin', but he sometimes would come out of the camper dressed with three shirts on. Adren started in about 1989 but was hittin' us hard by 1992. We managed OK, but in 1992, as we were doin' the festival at the City, it seemed things finally were at their worst as Adren kept slippin' away from us. Initially, he slipped away from the camper in the middle of the night. It was eleven o'clock at night, and he was in the bed. He had got up to go to the bathroom and got lost. When I got up in the mornin', I noticed him gone. I went up to the shower room and had my little dog Luke with me. As I came back out, I heard steps comin' down the road. It was Adren. "What are you doin' out here?" I asked him. He replied, "I been walkin' out here all night." When we got to the camper he said, "I bet I passed this a dozen times." He had been walkin' for hours.

Then I got Stacy Davenport to help me work in the booth and I came home with Adren for two days. Stacy's dad got hurt, and he had to go home, so we alternated workin' the booth. I worked three days, and he worked two. My granddaughter-in-law, Darlene Hensley, looked after Adren at the City while I worked. He got away one time at the bathroom by goin' out a different door through the restaurant. Nobody stopped him, but directly, somebody brought him back up. They had found him at the turnstile after somebody recognized him. Right after we got back home from the City, Tim took Adren to look at some property they had purchased north of town. The girls had told Tim they thought their Dad was gettin' Alzheimer's, but Tim didn't see it. They got to the property and started walkin' over it. Just a short ways from the truck, Adren told Tim to go on and he would wait in the truck. About two hours later, Tim called me and said, "I've lost Adren." I said, "I could've told you not to let him out of your sight." Tim said, "I realize that now." I called my son Russell and his son Avery and they began to gather people to look for Adren. Later, a Mr. Halliday called me and said, "I have Adren out here." I said, "Hang onto him, and don't let him get away." In the meantime, we got a hold of some of the crew, and they went and picked him up. It was five hours from the time Tim and Adren left the house until they returned home.

Adren still insisted on drivin'. I was worried to death for him to drive. I couldn't say, "No you can't go." I could say, "Why don't you just stay here?" He had a little route that he took about once each day. He tore up the transmission in the truck, and so that ended the drivin'. I was afraid he would pull out in front of somebody. After the truck was out, he came and told me I was gonna have to take him to buy a car or let him drive mine. I told him, "I will drive you." We drove around to different car lots and came back. It was that night that he had a heart attack in June of 1993. At the time, I wasn't sure if that was what happened, but I called Sandy. With that Alzheimer's, I would ask if he was hurtin', but he just said no. Since he was up the next mornin', I thought he was OK, but he didn't eat anything all day. So I told him we would take him to the doctor the next day.

By the next mornin', he was becomin' increasingly weak as Sandy and me, one on each side, were tryin' to lead him to the car. She ran to call the doctor, and he collapsed from my grip onto the floor as the nurse was tellin' Sandy to call the ambulance. She said, "You call the ambulance!" and slammed the phone down. We coaxed him to crawl down the hall to the livin' room floor. We knew he would have to be taken by ambulance and the hall was too narrow for them to negotiate. He was taken by ambulance to the hospital where he stayed in intensive care for a week before they moved him to a private room. Later, we took him to the nursin' home where he stayed for four years. They had to watch him close, but even though they did, he got out sometimes. I could still drive my car and could go see him until I was legally blind. After that, I had a neighbor who would visit her mother-in-law in the same home and would take me almost every day.

I still continued my work with the City and did some traveling to perform. Me, my son-in-law, Tim Nelson; and granddaughter, Melodie Nelson; flew to Port Townsend, Washington, for the Festival of Fiddle Tunes on July 3, 1995. It was my first and only time to teach at a fiddle camp. I did a class a couple of times a day for five days. We did some performances on stage also. Some other participants were Brad and Linda Leftwich and Dan Gellert. Different styles of fiddle playin' like western, Irish, bluegrass, and old time fiddlin' were taught there as well as some other classes on other instruments. Guitarist Wayne Henderson was one of the other instructors.

I was never away for too long a period and I would be back visiting with Adren. He knew me all along, but he didn't know the kids after he had the heart attack. Sandy took me in, and we would question him. He recognized me right off. "You still got that little black dog?" he would say. We would take the dogs Luke and Rascal in sometimes. I would ask him if he knew Sandy, and he would say, "No, but she's a mighty pretty girl." Then, in a bit, after we told him, he seemed to remember. He knew me right up until a week before he died when pneumonia took him. He couldn't talk there for several days before he passed away on July 27, 1997. By that time, it wasn't as bad for me as it was when he had the heart attack. I didn't have an interest for anything and thought I would just have to quit everything after the heart attack. But after watchin' him, it was almost a relief to get him out of his sufferin'. Once it was over, it was very lonesome. It was hard to get use to it. He was havin' such a hard time, but he was no longer hurtin'.

I just wanted to sit around, thinkin', "I ain't got him to talk to and to cook for." I had to get myself used to bein' by myself. I was kind of used to it by the time he passed away, but knowin' that he was really gone made a difference. I was alone all of sudden. I got to the point that I realized he wouldn't want me to sit down and do nothin'. He would want me to live my life as if he was here. I had to force myself to begin. Kids and friends came along, and that helped out a lot. I had a lot of encouragin'. I've still got the kids — they're my children. I told myself, "I gotta live for the livin'. Perk up and be myself."

While I was helpin' Adren, I had little time to worry about my own health, but I was battlin' issues with macular degeneration. My vision was slowly slippin'. While I had relied upon my eyes to do all the work I had done — fiddle-makin', whittlin', sewin' — at a time when I really needed to throw myself into these efforts, I was findin' my ability to do the fine work now challenged. Even though my whittlin' had to come to an end, I could still see the shapes I carved displayed around my home. So I found myself mournin' on several fronts as time passed, but I held my head high and stepped for'ed knowin' that I still found comfort in the many talents God still afforded me and my family.

In the middle of August, Wonnie, her husband, and four children decided to move back to Arkansas. Tim said he wanted to move his kids near to me. They were gonna rent a house until they found a place to build. I told them there wasn't any use to rent, that they could move in with me. They took me where I needed to go, and Tim was my back-up at the City durin' the next two Fall Festivals givin' Sandy a break. My grandson Sterling Flagg eventually backed me up in 2009, 2010, and part of 2011. One of our favorite jamming events for the past thirty-two years was the Arkansas Fiddlers Convention at Harrison, Arkansas, each March. I have only missed one of those and always find an opportunity to learn something new.

Violet and Adren Hensley perform in 1990.

Violet and Adren Hensley in 1987 at Silver Dollar City.

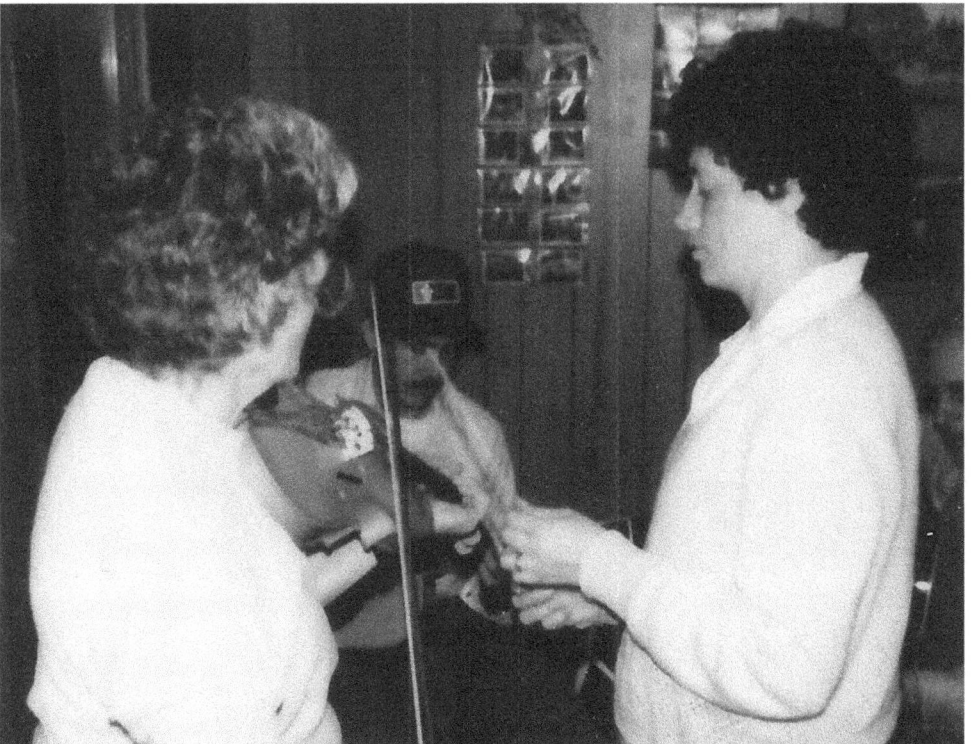

Violet Hensley and Sandra Flagg play with fiddle sticks in 1987.

In front of millions

While one might expect time to pass you by as you get older and older, thanks to the gifts shared with me as a youth, I still managed to keep relevant with the folks who made popular culture popular.

One day at the house, when I was seventy-four years old, I received a call from a lady wantin' me to go on David Letterman's show. They asked me what I did and I, of course, explained about makin' fiddles and playin'. Instead of David Letterman they decided they wanted me for "To Tell the Truth" hosted by Alex Trebek. They told me how much they would pay me, and all I had to do was come to the airport and fly to Los Angeles, and a man would be there holdin' up my name. Sure enough, they were true to their word. They picked me up in a limousine and loaded me in the back seat with some famous person that I can't remember and then dropped us both at the motel.

I was on the show with Erin Murphy, who played "Tabitha" on "Bewitched," and another lady who was supposed to look like her cat. They were settin' me up either as a senior prom queen or a fiddle maker and were pollin' the contestants. They prompted me ahead tellin' me, "You want to tell the truth, but don't give too much away," so I took my time with the answers.

There were three people on this bench to ask me questions about fiddle makin' and three people to ask me about bein' a senior prom queen.

Kitty Carlisle and Orson Bean were panelists along with a man named Dennis and a lady named Robin. Alex introduced me, and I said the two truths they could question me about: "I am a high school senior just voted queen of my senior prom." and "I am known as the Stradivarius of the Ozarks. I make and play my own fiddles."

The questions flew fast:

Kitty: When did you go back to school?

Violet: A couple of years ago.

Dennis: I was gonna ask — How many years were you held back? But I suppose Kitty's question would undo that. After the prom, are you planning to make out or something like that?

Violet: Well, not really. I think I will just go and get me more education.

Robin: What qualities got you voted the queen of prom?

Violet: I was voted in by the classmates. They put the names in a box and they drew the name, and that's how I became queen.

Orsen: I am not clear if the prom has happened yet, but these days, does your date bring you a gardenia for your wrist?

Violet: The prom hasn't been held yet.

Orsen: Do you expect a gardenia?

Violet: Possibly.

Alex: Now let's get to story number two that this woman is the Stradivarius of the Ozarks.

Kitty: What kind of wood do they use in your fiddles?

Violet: Maple, spruce.

Dennis: Where was Stradivarius from?

Violet: Italy.

Robin: How long does it take to make one of the fiddles?

Violet: About six weeks or so.

Orsen: What is the 'Devil's Dream'?

Violet: It's a fiddle tune.

Then they asked a girl, Pam Owen of West Covina, California, in the audience to judge what I was.

Pam Owen: "Well, she's really got me stumped, but I am going to say she's the prom queen."

Alex: Violet Hensley, what is your true story?

Violet: I make and play fiddles.

Alex asked me if we could take a look at one of my fiddles, and I told him I cut the tree I made the fiddle out of. I played a little tune — "She'll

Be Comin' 'Round the Mountain" — and the audience joined in clappin' in time as I played it up on my shoulder, a-clog dancin', and then raised it up over my head and never missed a beat. Even though she missed it, she got a prize, and I got $1,000. The show aired April 14, 1991.

By the next winter, I was headed to the center of television for the east coast. This time, we went to New York City for me to appear on the popular mornin' show "Live! with Regis and Kathie Lee." It was on February 2, 1992, that I began another trip for Silver Dollar City. Lisa Rau of the City made the trip with me. I took my fiddle makin' and my little hatchet to show how I chopped on the wood. I carried the axe and some tools and fiddle parts with me in a little silver brief case on the plane. That would never happen today.

We had to be into the studio by 11 a.m. on February 3. They were celebratin' senior week, so I guess I qualified. Kelly Coffield (who later became known as Kelly Coffield Park) was the other guest who was on before me. Regis brought me out and announced to the audience, "An amazing seventy-five-year-old great-grandmother that not only plays the fiddle but makes the fiddle as well." They put my fiddle makin' and my pieces of wood and my number four and number fifty-six fiddles on a rolling table. I came out with Regis and Kathie Lee who were standin' behind the table, and they started askin' me questions. One would ask a question, and then the other: What kind of woods? What did I sell them for? How long does it take to make one? When did I make my first one? He asked me what happened to my first fiddle, and I told him. I was out huntin' squirrels when I found it had been stomped all to pieces. It was around about 1948 when I found the fiddle broke up. Some years later I found out Russell and RG had broke it when they couldn't get music out of it — they were about six and eight years old. He said, "You went squirrel hunting?" I said, "Yeah, we had to have somethin' to eat!" and everyone laughed.

Kathie Lee asked a question that spurred my comments about makin' and repairin' things such as churn lids, plow handles, and wagon tires. Jokingly, Regis asked me "How about a shower?" He got us all to laughin' includin' me as I replied, "We didn't have a shower." He said he was tryin' to find somethin' that was not made with wood. Eventually, we meandered back to fiddle makin' and fiddlin'. After a short description of makin', Regis said, "Let's see how they sound." I picked up my fiddle, and number four was out of tune, so I had to change fiddles. Then I did a little dance while playin' "She'll Be Comin' 'Round the Mountain." I was gonna show Regis how to play; he was just a little taller than me. He said, "I got no talent at all." I told him to tuck the fiddle under his chin, and I helped him draw the bow across a lick or two and sang "Daddy ate a hot dog." Then he repeated it and stomped his feet up and down like he was dancin'. Regis is real funny, a jolly man that could easily think of things that make people laugh. The show was well-received, and they actually ran that clip again. They gave me $500 for my appearance.

I remember that the prices in New York were out of sight. A cup of coffee in the hotel was eighteen dollars. I brought home a list of prices. They took me to a sushi bar to eat. When they brought me a piece, I said, "That fish needs to go back in the creek." I couldn't eat raw fish, so I had fried chicken. When we started to fly back, they checked my silver brief case, and the man wouldn't let us carry it anymore. As they started to take my hand axe out and keep it, Lisa argued with them, tellin' them I had to have that to make fiddles. One of the men with the airline carried it and put my briefcase in the luggage compartment. When we came back to Springfield and dropped off one of our party at the TV station, sportscaster Ned Reynolds came out to the car where I was waitin', sayin' he had always wanted to meet me. That, of course, was a nice surprise since my appearances on the station were never scheduled when he was on for the news.

My next excursion was for the Disney Channel, but it was just as far as my livin' room when they came to interview me on December 4, 1992, for the show, "Making Their Mark." The show featured seniors that did all types of activities of interest from blues drummer Chris Columbo in Atlantic City, to a man who built a telescope to look at the moon, to another eighty-two-year-old woman that took children on hikin' trips. They set up in the livin' room with a four-person crew and one of the grandsons, Deven Porter, got to help by holdin' up one of the mics or light poles. They had me play a little bit and interviewed me about fiddle makin'.

On one of my TV excursions, I got to appear with Country Music Hall of Fame member Ralph Emery. One of the most-watched shows on cable television at one time was "Nashville Now with Ralph Emery" on The Nashville Network (TNN). Don Richardson took me down to appear on that show. They taped it inside the Gaslight Theater at Opryland theme park. I really enjoyed the evenin'. Unlike on so many of the other shows, I was among country pickers and singers. Though it was still a pretty big deal, I felt at home. Ralph talked a bit about Silver Dollar City and then brought me out to perform sayin', "This performer whittles fiddles and fiddles what she whittles." Then I went over and joined Ralph, and he questioned me about what kinds of woods I used in the fiddles. He asked, "Now tell me, do they just keep gettin' better with age?" I replied, "Up to a certain point, then like you, they just level off." The reaction to the comment was so great from the audience that Don and all the folks backstage heard the laughter. He just laughed and couldn't say anything for a little bit, then said, "I leveled off five years ago." I played "Take Me Back to Tulsa" with the Nashville Now staff band. After we finished, they brought out Randy Robbins, the son of Marty Robbins, who was pursuin' a singin' career. I remember him turnin' to me and sayin', "Oh good, I get to sit by you."

Silver Dollar City publicity person Lisa Rau took me up to the Michael Felbin Show in Springfield in 1996. Another artist who became a mainstay of Branson in his later life, singer and TV personality Andy Williams (1927-2012), was also on the show with me. It was a pleasure to meet and share the stage with Andy there.

I did annual promotional appearances for the city until 1986, and then we pared back to intermittent TV appearances until 1996. Since that time, the City has brought the media to me rather than me going to them. I am still honored to speak in any medium to tell people about the great things we do at Silver Dollar City and the wonderful gifts that have encouraged me throughout my life. While finishing this book in 2014, I am preparing for my forty-eighth fall festival at Silver Dollar City at this year's National Harvest and Cowboy Festival. It seems that the years have just flown by as I have watched our once small attraction become one of the biggest amusement parks in the country to include one hundred acres of fun things that a family can do together. My tasks for the City have remained unchanged from year to year, although my craft and performance area in the park has moved from time to time.

Through most of the years, many of us camped nearby, and, like family, we have worked side-by-side year end and year out. As years progressed, the actual length of the fall festival featuring crafts has lengthened sometimes to as much as two months, providing us about thirty-two days of work. I remained in the Gazebo for my first nine festivals displaying my talents.

When we came to the City, there was a blacksmith shop, a general store, an ice cream parlor, a doll shop, two log cabins, the McHaffie homestead, and the Wilderness Church. In our spare time, my family and

I enjoyed the early rides offered: the stagecoach, the train, the diving bell, and the float trip. As the park expanded and added new adventures, we always were willing to give them a try. I understand about a half-million folks visited each year in my early days, and the craft festivals were always a big attraction.

The folks that I have met through the years have been so great to me, and many have become friends with some even remembering me at Christmas and birthdays. Each and every person I have met over this near half century brought something into my life. I am told that the park has welcomed seventy-one million visitors with most of those being during my association with the City. It is safe to say that I cannot remember them all and all cannot remember me either, but I have seen days when folks were as thick as hair on a dog's back. I will mention one couple, who in many ways represent all the great friends — Ray and Lyda Arnold of Overland Park, Kansas. I met them my first year along with their girls. Through the years they would visit, and when they stopped coming their daughters would bring their children who are now grown as well. I have entertained generations of families through my time at the City.

The City added "Jeanie" shacks or booths in about 1976, named after Jeanie Nichols, the craft coordinator at the time. I was moved to one of these shacks near the leather shop, and in 1979-80, I moved in the wagon works barn near the children's playground. I displayed in a booth at the back end of the basket shop beginning in 1981 where I remained for about a decade.

The show must go on, and never was this truer for me than in 1989. I was camping in my 1957 camper and driving my car back and forth to home and between the camp and the park. I was diagnosed with polymyalgia rheumatica, an inflammatory disease affecting the shoulders, neck, upper arms, and hips. My shoulders and hips had never hurt so bad. The doctor gave me four pills to take each day to make it through, and I made it. A person told me to take some exercise, and one night I lay in the floor of the camper and found I couldn't get back up. I liked to never got back on my feet. That festival was a two-month-long one, and at times I wondered whether I could go on. I would tell the visitors I was gonna be runnin' before the festival is over; that I couldn't stay this way; that I had to get better.

By the time the festival was over, I could run.

I was mainly stationed near the blacksmith shop through the 1990s and 2000s. The City made adjustments to different locations the last three years that take into account my advancing years and the impact the weather might have upon me. I continue to enjoy greeting and sharing my talents.

The City decided in 1981 that I would also begin appearing at the music festival each June for nine days in the midtown area of the City, with my first year performin' as a solo as a roamin' musician. I would just walk through and sit down on a bench and start playin'. By the second year, Adren and Sandy were appearing with me in forty-five-minute intervals alternating with other acts on specific stages in the park. One man shared with me in 1992 that he drove 2,000 miles just to hear me play "Walk Along John." In 1993, they asked me to also have a booth during the music festival. We did the music festival for twenty years until 2002 when the City revamped the festival and our focus was once again the fall festival with added music.

It was in May 2001 we were workin' in front of the Glassblower's shop that I started hurtin' while performin' durin' the music festival. The pain was down my right side to my knee. I paid it little mind and just kept playin'. My grandson Scott Hensley was gettin' married in Temple, Texas. So the City found out I wasn't goin' and they insisted I go. So I did, and they let me turn the show over to Sandy and George during the last three days of the festival. I rode to Temple with Russell. It was a miserable trip, and I had to keep loosenin' my seatbelt as we went. I came back with Tim and Wonnie, and then I went to the doctor who gave me pills to take at home for the pain and return in two weeks. Sandy and Wonnie decided about halfway that they were taking me to the emergency room. Finally, I agreed. They did some tests that went to the doctor, and I returned on the appointed day. When I went back, the doctor was not happy with what he was seeing in the tests and sent me in for a sonogram. The doctor at the hospital doing the test said, "If she had not been hurting for a month, I would have her in surgery right now." In the morning, they gave me a little shot, and the next thing I knew Sandy said "She's awake." And I replied, "I ain't been nowhere yet." They said, "You done had your surgery." My appendix had burst in May, and somehow it had managed not to kill me despite the passage of so many weeks.

Through the decades, the City got bigger and added many different rides and attractions with up to 22,000 people coming in one day to enjoy our offerings. Where there were once just a handful of crafters, now there are over one hundred and twenty-five creating beautiful things of all shapes and varieties.

Photo: Silver Dollar City

Violet Hensley visits with Alex Trebek on the set of "To Tell the Truth."

Left: Violet Hensley appears on "Live! with Regis and Kathie Lee"
Below: Violet teaches Regis Philbin how to play a tune on the fiddle.

When Glen Campbell opened his Goodtime Theater in Branson in 1994,
he and Silver Dollar City legend Violet Hensley promoted
tourism to Branson together.

Violet Hensley and
Glen Campbell join
Sandra Flagg's
family. From left are
Beverly, Amanda,
Fred, Sandra
holding Sterling,
and Aaron in 1994.

Fiddlers Shoji Tabuchi and Violet Hensley visit in Branson in 1990.

Below: Charlie Hardin, Sandra Flagg, Violet Hensley, Adren Hensley, and Betty Supinger playing on Midtown Stage at Silver Dollar City in 1985.

Branson personalities Boxcar Willie and Violet Hensley pause for a photo in 1996.

Ricky Skaggs and Violet Hensley visit backstage in 1996.

Awards and accolades

So many across the world anxiously awaited the arrival of the new millennium. I did too ... I guess ... but my concerns weren't about computers failin' and passin' our world back into the pre-computer age. That was where I was livin' anyway. I didn't have one and still do not. I guess the saddest part of the 2000s was once again hearin' about our country bein' attacked as terrorists destroyed the Twin Towers in New York City on September 11, 2001. But, much like the rest of America, once the initial shock was passed, it was back to everyday tasks and continuin' my work. There were also concerns for my grandson, Matthew Nelson, who would have to do two tours of duty in Iraq and one in Afghanistan as a result of the War on Terror that followed.

It was in this decade that I began bein' honored by those who thought I had done somethin' worthy of recognition in my life. That same fall as the sadness of 9/11 settled over America, we were back at Silver Dollar City workin' to lift the spirits of those that wished to find the heart of America still alive and pumpin'. In this year, my many years of sharin' my talents there earned me an induction into the Silver Dollar City Hall of Fame. They had given me their Living Treasure Award in 1997. The accolades they have presented to me mean so much because the folks there are really family to me and mine. If it weren't for Silver Dollar City, there would have been no reason for anybody except my loved ones to say, "boo" about Violet Hensley.

Mayor Janell Kirkwood of Yellville nominated me to be among those considered for the Living Treasure of Arkansas in 2004. When it all started, I didn't have much interest in it because I didn't know what it was all about. Sandy, Sister, and Wonnie wanted me to gather everything up — information about what I had done, all the interviews, articles, performances, and people I had taught. I really didn't want to do all that. I didn't know what it was for, and they didn't tell me why. The mayor finally came and told me why all that was needed.

The experience culminated in a big event with music and refreshments at the Yellville-Summit School auditorium on May 15 where folks from Little Rock came and presented the Living Treasure Award to me. I didn't really feel like I had earned such an award. Other people had built me up. I didn't feel I done anything to get an award. It sure didn't make me feel like I was better than anybody else. But I was pleased just the same.

I was honored when Alice Gerrard of North Carolina invited me to come and perform at MerleFest in Wilkesboro, North Carolina. She, along with Brad Leftwich and Tom Sauber, were playin' out at Mountain View and came to stay with me, and we played and played for about a day and a half. I don't think we missed a tune. I would end up goin' there twice. The first time was in April 2004. Sandy and I played on the Traditional Stage that later Doc Watson would play on. They also had me, Sandy, and Wonnie play at the Traphill Elementary School and on the Americana Stage. On the Americana Stage we played with Etta Baker, a ninety-four-year-old black blues player who performed with a banjo and electric guitar. She had been playin' since she was about five years old. I played on another stage, sponsored by Homespun Tapes, with several fiddlers all lined up. Some of the players were Darrell Anger, Stuart Duncan, Karen Evans, and Brad Leftwich. We took turns playin' a tune and talkin' about our fiddlin' style. When it was my turn, I said, "I want to know if anyone can do this." I started to play, "She'll be Comin' 'Round the Mountain" with my fiddle on my head and dancin' at the same time. Stuart Duncan played his between his legs like a cello, and some of the other fiddlers started tryin' to do tricks. Darrell Anger tried several times to bring them back to demonstratin', but they were all havin' too much fun. Finally, he started hoppin' around playin' his, too. The workshop was considerably different than what it was intended to be. It certainly was not borin'. A man asked me if I had lived in Yellville all my life, and I said, "No, I'm sittin' right here."

The second time we went was in 2009. This time Tim and Wonnie backed me up at Miller's Creek Christian School. I played on the Traditional Stage again. This time it was a variety show with singin' and cloggin'. Brad and I both played fiddles and played "Waltz of the Violets" and "Shortnin' Bread." Then Tom Sauber, who plays a banjo, and I, did "Walk Along John" and "Black-Eyed Susie." Other folks were demonstratin' their style of clog dancin', and I did the mule dance.

The excitement over my next honor really got me to dancin' as we headed to Memphis for the Folk Alliance International Conference in 2009 where I received the Mike Seeger Scholarship. Mike was a talented musician who was part of the New City Ramblers. He focused so much of his life on studyin' old-time music. Matt Brown, a fan of mine, nominated me for this distinction. They brought me to their conference to share some of my experiences and music. When they had me up on stage playin', Tracy Schwarz, also a member of the New City Ramblers, called out to ask if I still played "Uncle Henry." I met him originally in Washington, D.C., when I was performin' at the National Folklife Festival and I played that tune. He liked it and asked me to tape it for him to learn. So I did, and mailed it. And he was supposed to send some tunes in exchange. Fifteen years later, he read an article about me and remembered to send me a tape of his tunes. It was good to see him again after forty years; I recognized his voice when he spoke up from the audience. He had his fiddle with him, so he came up on stage and joined me, and we played the tune together.

The honors kept rollin' as we rang in a new decade. I never really thought of what I did as bluegrass. In a way sometimes it was though, if you look at the instrumentation I recorded with. The International Bluegrass Music Museum in Owensboro, Kentucky, hosted a series of events to honor the pioneers. I was excited to be invited to join the group and be honored alongside a large group of distinguished names in bluegrass music in 2010. I felt pleased to be there, but I didn't know if I really belonged because I never played with any of them. They called me a legend just because of this type of music I did. At the event, I performed a show with my son-in-law Tim Nelson and my grandson Sterling Flagg. I got to visit with members of Bill Monroe's Blue Grass Boys as well as Hall of Fame member Curly Seckler, and Medicine Show legend Ramblin' "Doc" Tommy Scott. I love Bill Monroe's music. It was a great experience bein' included amongst these people who, like myself, have reached out to so many with the talents God gave. I was very honored.

As I rattle off these distinctions, I don't want to diminish how I feel about receivin' these, but let me put these recognitions into prespective. I spent a life makin' fiddles and playin' fiddle tunes. I didn't invent a cure for the common cold, although my chicken dumplin's come close. I didn't find a new way to power all these gadgets that folks like to have around to make life easier, but I do see the merit in gettin' things done the old fashioned way. I didn't create a product that everyone has to have, although many have wanted my fiddles or somethin' I whittled. What I did do was raise and care for a family with love, overcomin' obstacles I have mentioned and some I didn't. I loved one man throughout my life with my only other passions bein' in the wood I whittled and the music I created from those pieces of wood I put together. While it is almost impossible to know exactly how many I created, it is safe to say I have encouraged tens of millions of smiles in my life. That, my friends, is the greatest award or accolade any entertainer can claim.

I know it is mine.

Violet Hensley receives the Arkansas Living Treasure Award in 2004.

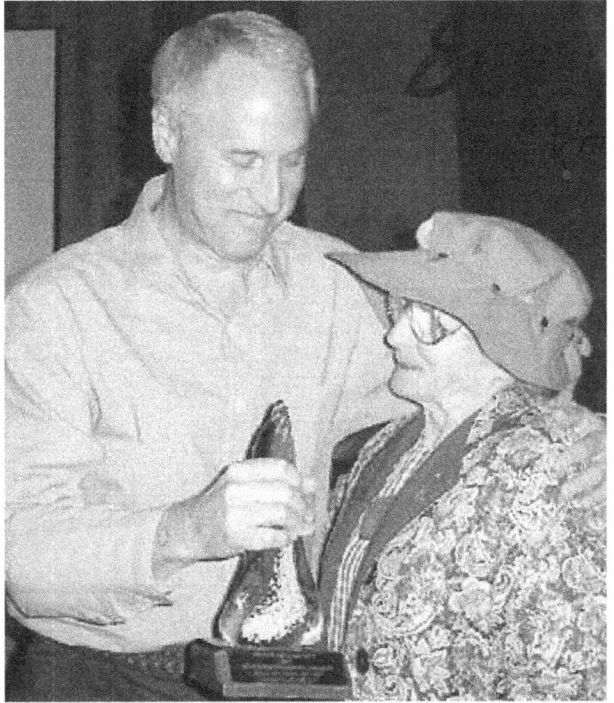

John Baltes inducts
Violet Hensley
into the
Silver Dollar City
Craft Achievement
Hall of Fame
at Silver Dollar City
in 2001.

Violet Hensley visits with fellow folk artist Doc Watson (1923–2012)
at MerleFest in 2004.

Violet visits with blues guitarist Etta Baker (1913–2006) at MerleFest in Wilkesboro, North Carolina, in 2004.

Photo: Betse Ellis

Violet shows some Silver Dollar City patrons her talents in 2008.

Violet jams in Memphis where she received the Mike Seeger Scholarship.

Violet visits with Brad and Linda Leftwich at MerleFest in 2009.

Violet Hensley entertains Silver Dollar City
visitors at her booth in 2011.

Violet Hensley performs with Betse Ellis (left) Sandra Flagg, and Sterling
Flagg at the Rock House in Reeds Spring, Missouri, on March 17, 2013.

A few parting thoughts

I want to thank each of you who have taken the time to walk along beside me through this adventure of reflectin' upon my life. I hope that there is somethin' within that brought a smile to your face, inspired you to do somethin' with your life that encourages others, or simply offers the joy in doin' what needs to be done in raisin' your family or carin' for your old folks. Hard work never hurt anybody.

I have been blessed to make it to ninety-seven with a great deal of independence despite the ailments of age that limit me. Even today as I pick up a piece of wood, though I can't see it clearly, I can almost feel the beat of the heart of a horse within it wantin' to gallop to life. I got a piece of butternut wood when I was nearin' the end of my whittlin' work, I saw four or five horses in there, but I never got those started. Each time I pass it, I can almost hear their whinny. How I wish I could help them find their footin'.

Why did I whittle and fiddle? Maybe it was the desire to create somethin' that others might find beautiful. I certainly had many who sought after my creations and smiled at my efforts no matter how simple or detailed. For me though, I think each endeavor brought a few moments of peace when I could tune out the sounds of the world around me as I found myself starin' into a piece of wood seekin' to reveal the secrets within or bringin' the tunes in my head to life and strivin' to reveal those to the world.

I owe a great deal of thanks to my children who give so much of their time back to me and make sure that the things I can no longer do are done. No matter what I said within these pages, know that I still think I shared a life and work with a wonderful man and was blessed with a wonderful family.

I am thankful that God gave me such a long life, the opportunity to see such miracles, and live such adventures. My secret to a long, wonderful life is this — live clean, never overindulge, don't drink, don't smoke, be yourself everyday, live as Jesus taught by lovin' your neighbors, and don't get to thinkin' you are better than anybody else.

One other bit of closin' advice — choose a path that you love and would love for others to follow, and then stick with it. Live each day the same. Don't let fame or fortune sway you to take the wrong path. I hope to see each of you one day around God's throne. I will be the one with the fiddle on top of my head playin' and dancin' for Jesus.

Photo: Betse Ellis

Appendix

Violet encourages her fiddle makin' students to add their own flair to creations through ornate fiddle scrolls: (clockwise from top) Ashlie Hueter's oak leaf scroll; George Flagg's wolf head scroll; and Violet Hensley's lion head scroll.

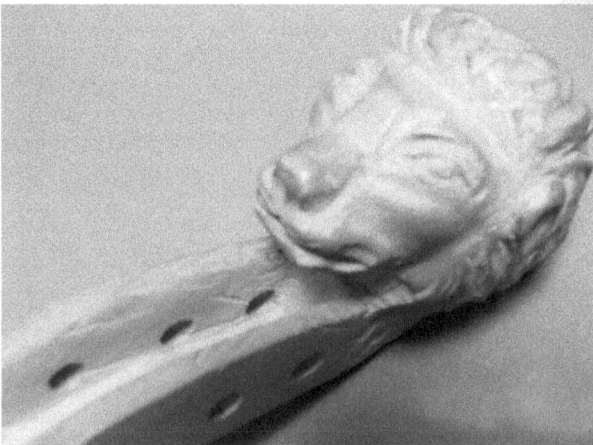

Violet has made seventy-two fiddles and one viola and rebuilt or repaired 438 violins. She taught fourteen students how to make fiddles, and has demonstrated the process for millions on television, at craft fairs, and Silver Dollar City. Among her students are four of her family members who continue the tradition.

Fiddle makin'

Teachin' each student the art of fiddle makin' happens right at the heart of my kitchen … the kitchen table! When makin' fiddles, I instruct students to use my measurements and guides to cut the fiddle molds, sides, front, back, neck, and smaller pieces. Then I go through each procedure and individually teach each student how to sand, bend, trim, carve, glue, and shape each section of the fiddle.

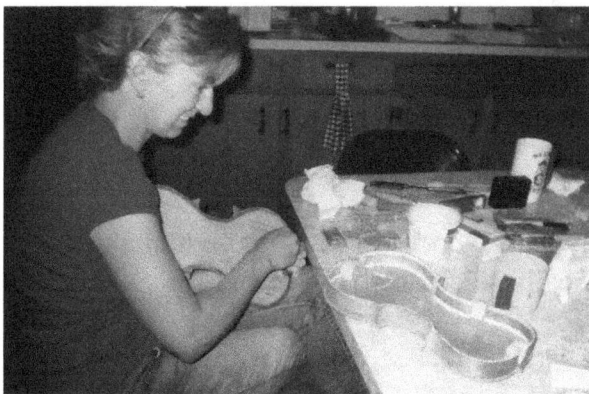

Ashlie Hueter receives a fiddle making lesson.

All sections of the fiddle are handmade usin' only special knives, scrapes, sandpaper, pocket knives, broken glass, and files. The finished project from beginnin' to end takes 260-plus hours. Each fiddle is unique, offerin' its own specialized tone, size, and personality.

First, I teach students what tools to use and how to use them.

Tools to have access to:

Drill press or hand drill;

Planer or edger (or someone who will plane it for you, or purchase pre-planed)

Band saw, keyhole saw, or similar small saw

Hand ax and chopping block

1/8" drill bit, 1/4" drill bit, 1/16" bit

Files — half round, round, square, triangular, and flat

Rasps for fast wood removal

C-clamps large and small

Clamps made from dowel rods or old thread spools (four-inch threaded bolt with wing nuts)

Clothespins, binder clips, bulldog clips, or alligator clips

Knives — Pocket knives and curved knives, sharpening accessories

Small chisels

Scrapes and/or sharp broken glass

Sand paper — coarse and fine

Glue — yellow wood glue and hide glue

Tru-oil (used for gun stocks) or finish of your choice

Flannel cloth or other polishing fabric

Keyhole reamer

Purfling tool (I use my pocket knife with a very small blade.)

Rim press (also called mold or form)

Side bending irons (optional)

Patterns — neck with appropriate scroll, sidepieces, top, back, and keyhole placement

Woods:

Next you must select the type of wood you want to use to make the fiddle. Below are the ones I usually select from to use and the sizes of the larger pieces.

Top: Softwoods such as, pine, spruce, buckeye, bass, or fine-grained sassafras

Back: Hardwoods such as any variety of maple or wild cherry

Solid top and solid back — Nine inches wide, fifteen inches long, at least 5/8 inches thick piece of wood

Two piece top or back — Two pieces, each five inches wide, fifteen inches long, at least 5/8 inches thick, glued together

Grain goes top to bottom of instrument.

Sides or ribs: Hardwoods such as any variety of maple or wild cherry (matching wood of back and neck)

One piece of wood ten inches long, one and 1/8 inches thick, three to four inches wide

Enough wood to cut nine strips slightly over 1/16 inch thick

Neck: Hardwoods such as any variety of maple or wild cherry (matching the back) nine inches long, two inches thick and three inches wide

You want the grain to run from heel of neck to the head along the nine-inch length.

Tailpiece: Purchased ready-made ebony or made of seasoned dogwood

Five to six inches long, 5/8-inch thick, two inches wide (Paper Pattern)

Fingerboard: Purchased ready-made ebony or make of walnut

Three inches wide, 1/2-inch thick, ten inches long

Endpin: Purchased ready-made ebony or make of a hardwood

One and 1/4-inch long piece and 1/2-inch square

Pegs: Purchased ready-made ebony or persimmon

Slab 1/2-inch thick, two to three inches wide, twelve inches long

Rim press: Oak

Two strips one and 1/8-inch thick, six inches wide, twenty-one inches long

Step One — Makin' a Mold

After teachin' a student about the tools, and selectin' woods, I tell each to choose the woods he or she desires. Then we begin the process of learnin' how to make the mold. The mold is used to form the ribs, so it must be the size and shape of the finished fiddle sides. The mold consists of four pieces: two outside halves and two inside halves. I call this mold a rim press.

A rim press is made from two oak boards that are one and 1/8-inch thick, six inches wide, and twenty-one inches long. See diagram for refer-

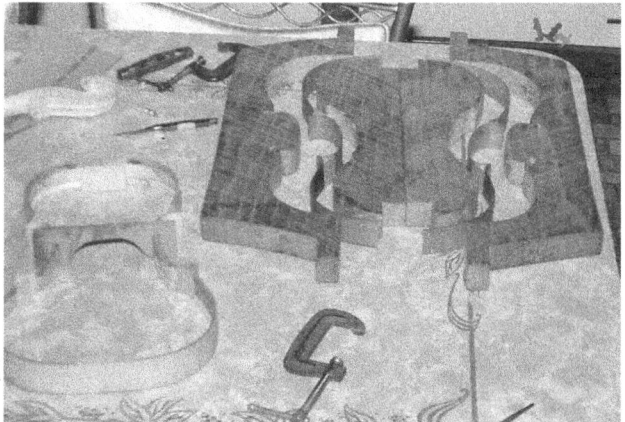

An oak rim press

ence.

Take a half fiddle pattern and draw it on one piece of this oak wood. Drill a 3/8-inch hole past the point of each corner of fiddle outside of the drawn pattern.

Then saw the shape out with a band saw. Cut a notch one-inch square in both ends of each inside piece at top and bottom in the center (D). That gives you one inside piece and one outside. Sand the cut area smooth on both interior and exterior pieces. When the 1/16th inch sides are clamped between the two pieces, it should all be flush.

At the top and bottom of the outside pieces, cut a one-and-a-half by one-inch section protrudin' out, (E), to use for clampin' the complete rim assembly together after sides are bent. Repeat from start with other half pattern on the second piece of oak.

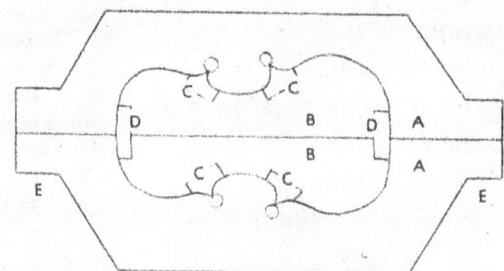

(Hint: Empty form pieces can be clamped together for storage by insertin' 1/16 inch thick wedges between the outside and inside pieces of both sides, then clampin' the ends together. The wedges will fill the width of the empty space required for the side-bendin'.)

A-Outside halfs
B-Inside halfs (about 1/8" smaller than inside of "A")
C- Opening to place corner blocks
D- Opening for End blocks
E-Neck of mold

A rim press diagram

Step Two — Makin' the ribs

Next, I teach the student to make and bend the sides, or ribs, usin' the hardwood of their choice. Cut one piece of wood — ten inches long, three to four inches wide, and one-and-one-eighth inches thick (the width of the side pieces).

With a band saw, cut eight strips from the one-and-one-eighth-inch edge of the wood block. (Each strip should measure ten inches long, one-and-one-eighth inches wide, and a generous one-sixteenth-inch thick to allow for sandin').

Sand all the strips smooth on both sides. Then clamp them together and sand the edges, so that the strips are exactly the same from end to end.

Unclamp, measure, and cut lengths to fit in the rim press. (Keep the drop-off pieces for wedges.) The front and big end pieces can be a little long; stickin' out of the press, because you can cut them to fit once everythin' is dry. The lengths of each section of ribs should match — two front, two center, and two big end pieces.

From the drop off pieces of wood, create two small wedges one-and-one-eighth inch by one-sixteenth inch thick, and roughly half inch wide, (the approximate distance from the outside of the drilled rim press hole to the inside rim press when side pieces, or one-sixteenth-inch wedges, are clamped in the press).

Photo: Sterling Flagg

Heat is added to rib sections.

Place the rib pieces in hot water until they are pliable, about fifteen to twenty minutes. You can do this in a pot on the stove. Take each piece out one at a time and place directly in the rim press or bend each around a bendin' iron.

Do one-half of the fiddle at a time. Separate the rim press into halves and use one half of the press.

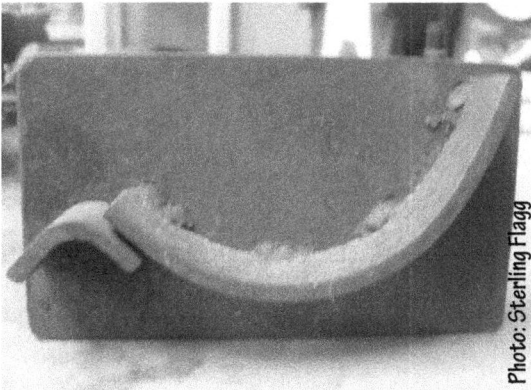

Photo: Sterling Flagg

Bending iron

When bendin' directly in the rim press (as I originally did), place the shortest sidepiece in the hole of the outer piece of the press half. Use a wedge to hold it in place, and bend it very gently and very slowly until it is in the other hole. Then use a second wedge to hold that end in place. This piece is the most difficult and is likely to break if done too fast or carelessly.

Select either a front or back end side piece. Remove the wedge and tuck one end in the appropriate hole, and gently place the inner portion of the form against the side piece and press it gently against the outer portion until it is tight. Use a C-clamp to hold it all together. The center and one end side piece are now sandwiched between the inner and outer portion of half the rim press.

Repeat the process usin' the third end piece.

Place a C-clamp in the middle of the two portions to hold it all in place.

Repeat the process for the other side. The ribs are set aside and allowed to dry for approximately twenty-four hours or more. The long ends will be trimmed later.

Now, when shapin' the ribs, I use bendin' irons, which were made for me. (See photo on 215)

I have one iron for each rib section. These irons are heated on the stove, then clamped in a vice. I then take a rib piece out of the water and bend it on the iron. Bend slowly or the wood will break and be careful not to have the iron too hot or it will burn the wood.

Once bent, trim and place the rib in the rim press in the appropri-

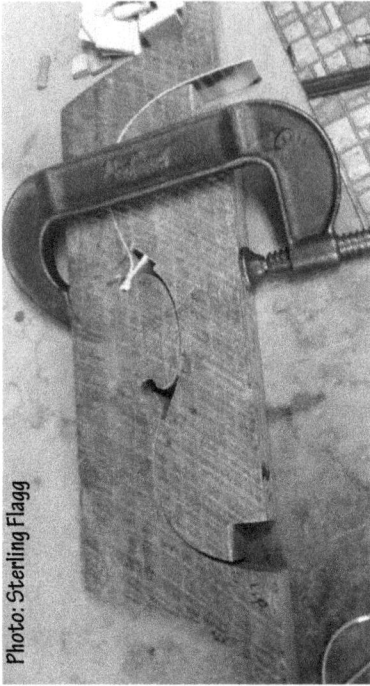

Photo: Sterling Flagg

One section of ribs is inserted in the rim press.

ate location. There is no need to hurry to clamp all the pieces together in the rim press because the wood is already dry and will stay in shape.

Repeat the process for all six pieces and then start with the rim press step as mentioned above without havin' to deal with the sides dryin'.

Step Three — The Neck

Students then must get a grasp on how to make a neck. The neck is shaped to the proper contour and then glued to the small

Photo: Sterling Flagg

Fiddle neck and scroll

end of the fiddle usin' a dovetail joint. It is made of hardwoods such as any variety of maple or wild cherry matchin' the back and sides.

Use one piece of wood — nine inches long, two inches thick and three inches wide.

While the ribs are dryin' the neck pattern can be drawn and cut out, usin' whatever scroll you have chosen: horse head, dog head, lion head, traditional scroll or one unique to the student.

The scroll design is drawn into the neck block.

Draw a basic pattern on the three-inch side of the block of wood includin' the area for scroll, neck, and heel. Saw just outside the pencil mark. The pattern should also show where the peg holes will be in the peg box. Mark the holes and drill with a one-fourth-inch bit all the way through before shapin' the cut block.

Then, draw a line in the center of the block from end to end and follow all the way around the piece of wood on both two-inch sides and both ends dividin' it in half.

Take a fingerboard or a fingerboard pattern and set on the topside of the block up to where the nut will set (about one-fourth inch from the bottom hole) and draw the shape from the heel to the scroll. It has to be centered on the block. Use a saw to cut away the excess wood outside the fingerboard lines from the nut down.

On the sides of the scroll section draw the circle for the center of the scroll and then draw the lines showin' the width of each level to be carved out.

A tiny saw can be used to cut away a portion of the wood on the ends of the scroll. Be sure not to cut deeper than the marks on the back and sides of the scroll section or the scroll will not be true or the sides will not match.

Horse head scroll

The heel and fingerboard taper towards

Photo: Sterling Flagg

Fiddle neck and scroll

the scroll so leave the scroll a little thicker.

Carve the neck with knives and/or chisels from the line on the back around to the front to the lines on the side of the scroll. These are dipped in slightly and sanded smooth.

Finish carvin' the back and sides and heel. In both areas use an existin' fiddle as a reference.

Start shapin' scroll with a very small pocketknife blade or scroll saw and the back of the neck, (handhold), and heel usin' a file or pocketknife and sandpaper it to make it smooth.

Mark and cut out the peg (key) box, it extends from the scroll to the nut. Use a chisel about one-fourth-inch wide or less to shape the inside of the box.

Also sand the smooth side of the neck where the fingerboard will eventually be glued.

Step Four — Continue working on Ribs and place Corner and End Blocks

Students next learn that every instrument must have somethin' solid to hold it together.

After the neck is carved, then return to work on the ribs. Select a section of ribs, remove the clamp, and trim the edges between the three pieces where the ribs connect. To glue the points together they have to be beveled so there will be an invisible seam.

The sides are then placed back in the press to retain their shape and to use as a guide for makin' the corner blocks to reinforce the corners when they get glued together.

Get a block of wood for corner block.

Corner and end blocks are reinforcin' blocks placed at the joints of the ribs to provide additional strength at critical points.

The blocks are made of bass wood, spruce, or soft pine. Each is fitted for its specific location in the violin. For the corner blocks, a three-fourths-inch square block of wood matchin' the height of the side, (about one-and-one-eighth inches), is required.

Make it into a triangular piece of wood long enough to fit in the corner block space of the rim press. The blocks are fitted by carvin', sandin' or filin' until it fits into the corner formed by the side pieces in the hole. These pieces have been trimmed to meet correctly to form the shape you want. (See photo on the next page.)

Once you have the block trimmed to fit, place a light coatin' of Elmer's wood glue on the two sides facin' the ribs. If too much glue is used, the ribs will glue to the rim press.

Use some small wooden wedges to hold the corner blocks in place within the rim press.

Repeat this process for the other half.

The glue generally dries in about two hours.

Once dry, trim the outside rib pieces even with the rim press so each will come together properly. Remove the C-clamps and bring the two halves of the rim press together. The big end has to fit with the cleanest seam since a slot will be cut in the other end to fit the neck in the body. C-Clamps are used to hold the entire form (four pieces) together at each end.

The mold is designed with a space at each end to allow the student to glue in the end blocks while the press is clamped together. That is the next step: make and glue in the end blocks. The end blocks are the same height as the sides and are about two inches wide and about three-fourths-inch thick and are carved and centered to fit snug against the seams where the sides are to join at each end of the fiddle.

Small wooden wedges will probably be needed to secure the blocks in place.

After the blocks are glued in cut away the sharp corners and round the blocks a bit.

Pocketknives, a half round or flat file, all are usable in this process.

Once again use glue sparingly and it will take about two hours for the end blocks to dry.

Step Five — Double liner

Now the student must learn about the double liner. The double liner is a second series of thin strips of wood glued on the inside edge of both top and bottom of the ribs to give more strength and body, to better glue the top and back to the ribs.

Use bass, soft pine or sassafras, one-fourth-inch wide, one-sixteenth-inch thick, and size strips to the length runnin' from block to block and around the inside edge of the fiddle.

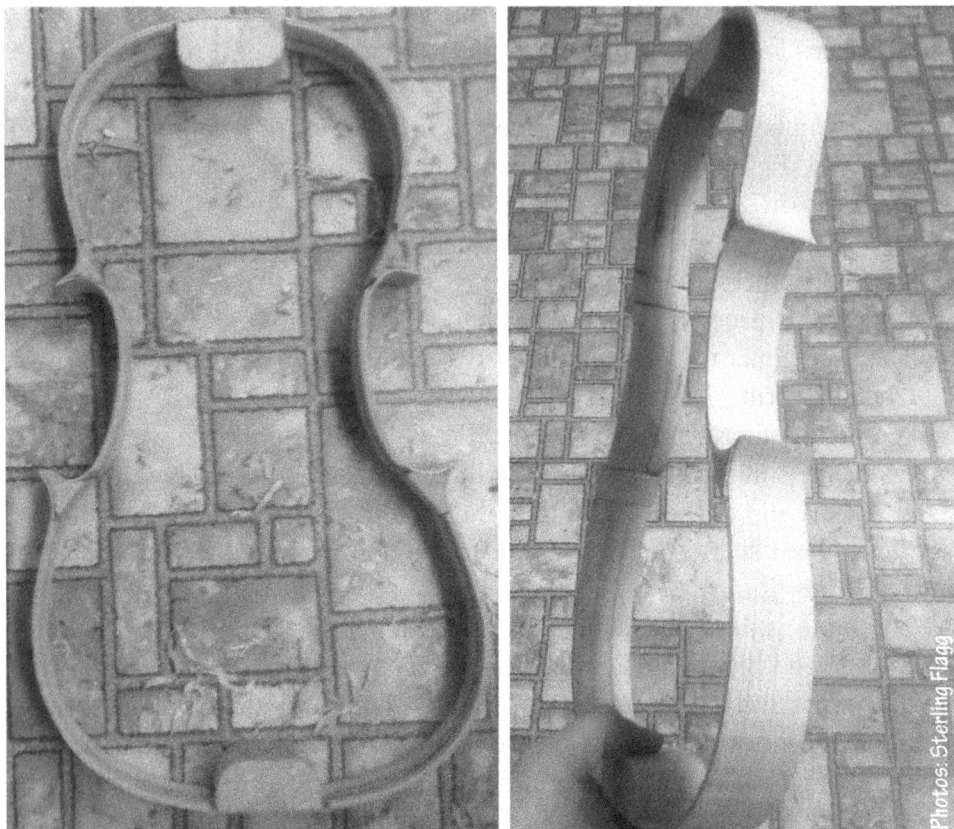

Photos: Sterling Flagg

Double liner with blocks

Place strips in hot water for five minutes so they will bend easily. Loosen the C-clamps holdin' the rim press together until the ribs slide about half way out of the press then tighten the clamps again.

Use wood glue to secure the six separate strips to the ribs between the end blocks and corner blocks. These strips are clamped into place usin' simple clamps: clothespins, alligator clamps, bulldog clips, or binder clips. Remember to put somethin' under the clamps, leather or wood, to keep the clamps from leavin' marks on the wood. (If any marks are left, dampen with water and allow it to dry. As it dries the grain will rise again. Sandin' may be necessary.)

After these strips are dried and clamps are removed, remove the middle pieces of the rim press and turn it over.

Push the ribs up and repeat process for the other side addin' six more pieces of double line. Sticks may be cut to press the form in shape while gluin' this section.

Step Six and Seven — Back and Front

Once this is done, I instruct students to use the sides as a pattern for makin' the back of the fiddle.

Top: Softwoods such as, pine, spruce, buckeye, bass, or fine-grained sassafras

Back: Hardwoods such as any variety of maple or wild cherry

Solid top and solid back: Nine inches wide, fifteen inches long, at least five-eighths-inches thick piece of wood.

Two piece top or back: Two pieces, each five inches wide, fifteen inches long, at least five-eighths-inches thick, glued together

Grain goes top to bottom of instrument

The back and front are generally made with two pieces of wood glued together, then usin' the ribs outline for a pattern, the front and back are rough cut to shape. The inside of both the front and the back are concave, while the outside is convex. The shapin' is accomplished by carvin' with a curved knife and with scrapers, both glass and metal. The top and back are approximately the same shape and use the same technique to carve and finish.

The back is done first.

After drawin' the shape on the wood, take the sides out of the rim press.

First place the sides on the boards matchin' the end joints of the sides to the center seam of the back and draw around the outside with a pencil. Then draw another line about one-eighth inch or a little more outside that line, givin' a little room for hang over.

Don't forget to leave a knob on the back to glue to the heel of the neck. Saw out the back usin' a band saw.

Then put your sawed out back on the chop block, and chip

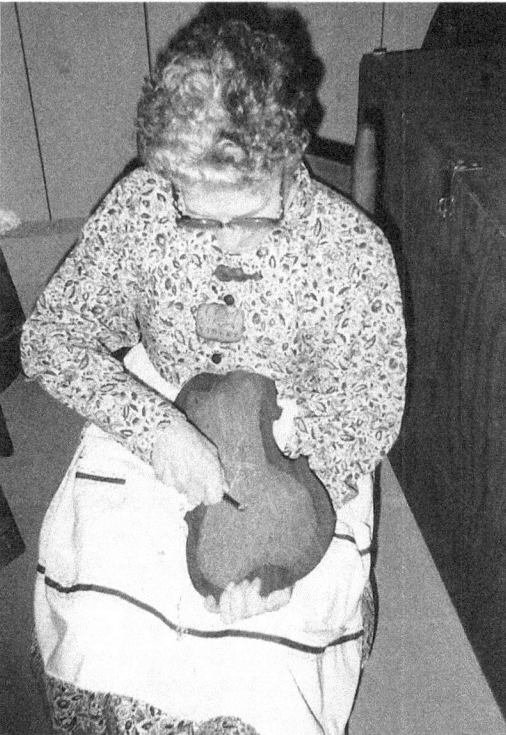

Violet Hensley carves at Silver Dollar City in 1991.

Above and Below: Violet Hensley uses an axe to shape a piece of wood in 1974 and 1994.

away excess wood with a hatchet. Place pin end on block and chop, taperin' from about three inches, leavin' the edge at least one-fourth-inch thick for finishin' by hand. Do the same with the neck end.

Be careful to keep it even, and not cut too deeply in any one place.

Next use a curved knife to shape the outside of the back by frequently referencin' a finished fiddle that is shaped in a way that is pleasin' to the student. It will gradually take shape as the student looks back and forth noticin' the differences between the two or they ask me to show or tell them where to cut next.

The inside of the back should have a line drawn about three-fourths inch from the edge all the way around. This is a guideline used to do the roughest work first and finishin' to the edge later. Begin carvin' with a curved knife and checkin' the wood thickness usin' a thumb on the inside of the fiddle top or back and a finger tip on the outside, or

the other way round, feelin' the depth of the wood as it is carved. This is done frequently especially as a lot of wood has been removed to retain the shape and to keep from carvin' through the wood and ruinin' the piece.

Remember to dip the top and back in slightly on the outside edge to help keep the clamps from slidin' off.

When the general shape is roughed out, begin usin' scrapes to smooth it and then last use different grades of sandpaper for the final finishin' touches. Start with coarse sandpaper and work down to fine.

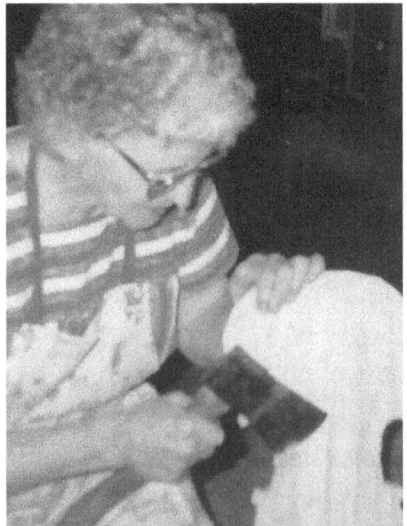

Fold it on a little block and use to level off high humps where whittled.

Always be referrin' to a finished violin, or me, checkin' details through the process.

Leave the bottom of the outside edge flat to glue to the sides.

Now get the ribs and completed neck. The student will place the neck against the center of the top end block of the fiddle and draw the edge outline of the dovetail slot in which it will be placed.

When lines are drawn, measure inside that line at least one-sixteenth inch and match a parallel line.

The cut will begin at the inside line and dovetail to the outside line reachin' about one-eighth inch deep into the block. Use a small saw to begin and cut out the remainder with a chisel or knife. Check throughout the process to make sure the neck will properly fit in the slot. Ultimately, the neck will rest with about three-eighths of an inch on top of the ribs.

If any of the heel of the neck sticks out the back with this measurement, it will need to be trimmed to fit flush with the bottom of the sides so the knob on the back can be glued.

It must be placed at just the right angle so the fingerboard will not be too high or too low.

When this process is finished, lay the neck aside, and then glue the back to the sides.

From a hardware store, the student should have acquired hide and hoof glue which is mixed with water and heated on the stove to prepare for use. When the

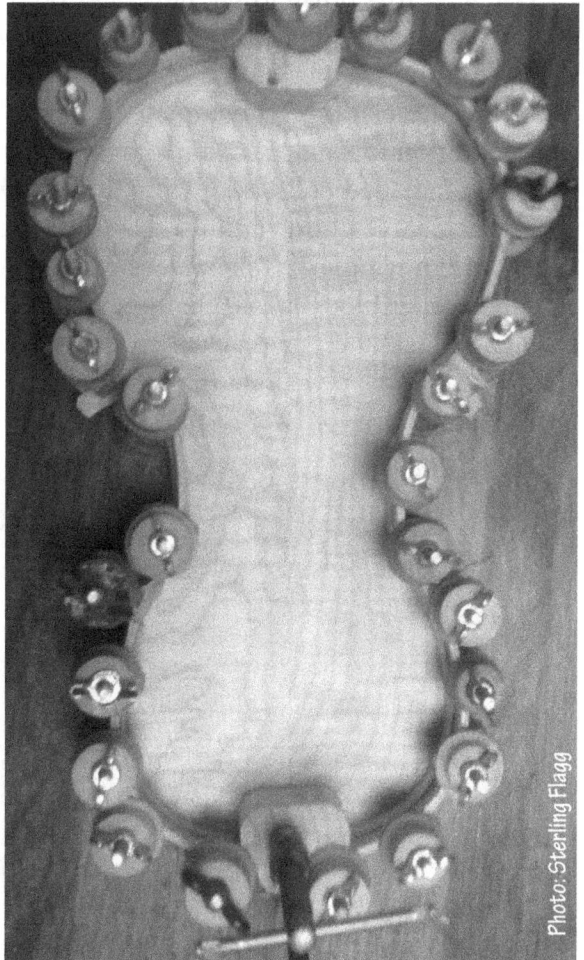

Glueing back to the sides

Photo: Sterling Flagg

Glue back to the sides

glue is tacky and will string between your thumb and fingers, it is ready.

Use a narrow brush to put hot water on the edge of the sides, includin' the blocks, then the edge of the back. Then with the brush apply the glue to the sides only. After glue is applied, drop the brush in water to soak for clean up after clampin' is complete.

In addition to small C-clamps, use clamps made from wooden spools, four-inch threaded bolts, and wing nuts. I saw the wooden spools in half, reverse the halves, slide a threaded bolt through each reversed spool, and fasten with a wing nut. Take pieces of wood or leather and lay over the end and corner block areas, clamp, then place two small C-clamps on each end block and one on each corner block. About twenty-two spool clamps can be placed along the remainder of the surface area of the back. Set aside and dry for twenty-four hours.

Items used in making a fiddle.

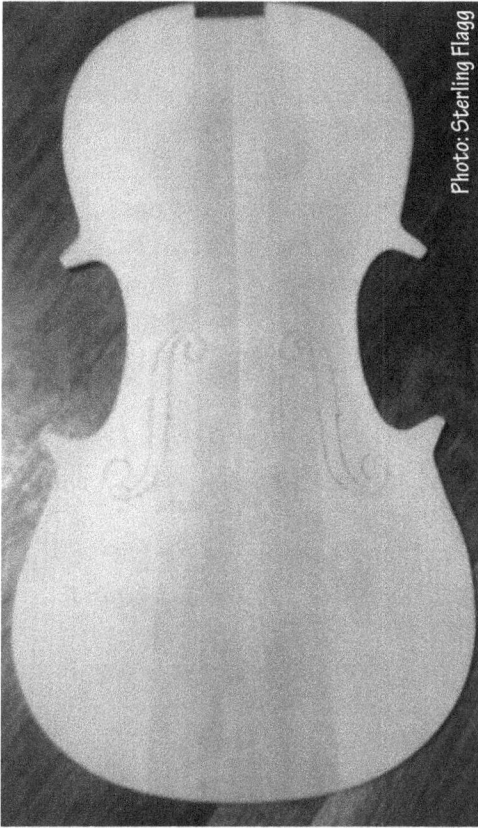

Photo: Sterling Flagg

Top with F-Hole design

When dry, remove clamps and draw the outline for the top usin' similar method as used for back. Once outlines are drawn then draw the shape of the neck dovetail on top, and then cut a notch to fit over the end of the neck.

Now, the neck can be glued in place. Use Elmer's wood glue or hide glue and place only on inside of back and inside the neck slot. Then slide neck in place. Put a C-clamp with a couple pieces of leather on the heel and the fingerboard edge, allowin' four hours to dry.

Then repeat the process used in shapin' the back to shape the front.

Once shapin' is complete, proceed to the next step.

Step Eight — Sound holes in front

Students are now taught how to enhance the top.

Take a pattern from an existin' instrument by shadin' with a pencil over the f-hole. Sound holes or f-holes should be cut into the appropriate location.

Placement will vary slightly on different instruments, but generally the bottom hole aligns just inside the lower corner block half-inch inside the edge of the top and the top holes will have about one-and-a-half inches space between the two f-holes. The center of the f-hole will be about three-fourth of an inch from the edge of the top.

Usin' a one-fourth-inch drill and a small saw to start and then use a small knife to achieve proper shape followed by sandin'. Use sandpaper on small dowel to sand out holes in each end.

Step Nine — Bass bar

The bass bar is a piece of bass, spruce or fine grain pine carved to fit the underside of the front, and is placed at an angle one-fourth inch from center line at small end and half an inch from centerline at large end. Carve the bass bar and fit it to the inside of the top where the bass strings will be. The bar is half an inch wide, one-fourth inch thick and seven inches long. The one-fourth-inch side of the bass bar will be fit to the left hand side of the top. Lay the bass bar where it will be glued and with a pencil mark the two sides and each end on the fiddle top so each time it is put back in the same place.

Also mark one end of the bass bar and always point it towards bottom of the fiddle. The bottom side of the bar must be a convex, fittin' the shape of the inside of the top. Use chalk on the back of the bar and it will rub leavin' a mark on the top to reveal high and low places on the bar that still need to be fitted to match perfectly. Then once shapin' is complete, glue in place with wood glue and clamp with C-clamps.

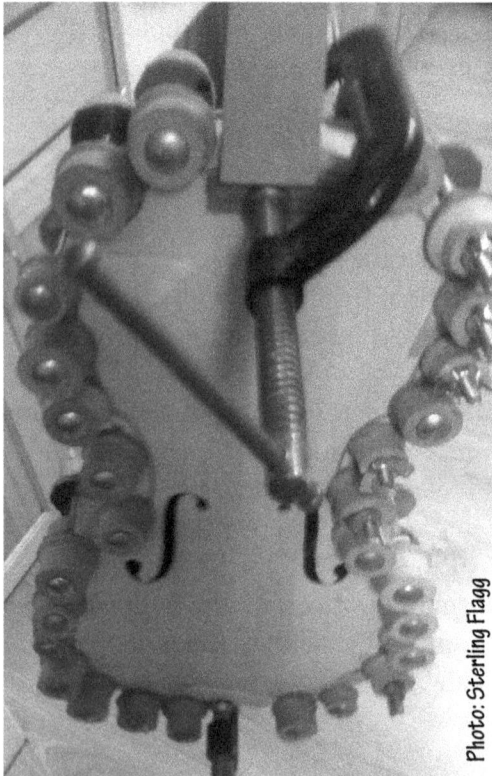

Photo: Sterling Flagg

Allow the bass bar to dry for about three hours. Then if solid, begin trimmin' the bar. About the middle of the f-hole the student should leave it high for about an inch or so and taper the bar to both ends to a featheredge. After that that the bar should be trimmed in the middle to where it is no less than five-sixteenths-inch high and then round off any square edges and sand the bar smooth.

Step Ten — Assembling the Front to the Sides

This is the same process as gluin' the back, usin' same clamps. Allow dryin' for twenty-four hours.

Glue top to the sides

Step Eleven — The Saddle

Now the student must add a saddle to the big end of the top, these can be purchased or made. The saddle is a small piece of hard wood that the tail line rests upon.

If made, use hard maple, hard walnut, persimmon or dogwood. A saddle is one-and-a-half-inches long, one-fourth-inch wide, and one-fourth-inch thick.

I prefer not to cut all the way through the top but only remove about half of the top's depth to place the saddle.

The saddle is about one-and-a-half-inches long. The center half inch will be about one-eighth inch higher than the top of the fiddle and the outer ends will taper until they are flush with the top when finished. Once ready, glue in place with wood glue.

Step Twelve — The Pegs

There are four pegs used for tunin' that hold the ends of the strings. These can be purchased or made. If made, use persimmon. It will take four pieces of wood, three inches long, half-inch thick and one inch wide. A peg shaper is a tool that can be purchased or the pegs can be made with a pocket knife and sandpaper.

Pegs have a knob on one end outside the pegbox and are tapered to the other end extendin' through the pegbox.

When the pegs are complete, I teach the students to use a keyhole reamer, which is tapered, to shape the key holes. Startin' in the first hole, nearest the nut, on the left side of the neck, use light pressure and cut just until the peg fits snugly on both ends. The next hole will ream from the right side of the pegbox. The next hole will ream from the left, and finally one more from the right.

There is a small hole drilled through the end of each peg that the string will be run through.

Mark a place to drill this hole by puttin' the peg in place and markin' just inside jaw of the fiddle on the little end of the peg. The hole is drilled with a small drill bit similar to the width of a G-string.

Violet Hensley adds pegs to a fiddle.

Step Thirteen — The End Pin

The endpin is a tapered wooden pin carved to fit in a hole on the end of the fiddle and anchor the tailpiece. The endpin may be purchased or made. If made, use ebony, hard maple, persimmon, or dogwood. Use a wood block one-half-inch square and one inch long. Refer to an existin' endpin to see shape.

Essentially the pin has two ridges that hold the tail wire in place when it is inserted in the end block.

Drill a hole with a one-fourth-inch drill bit in the center of the end block where the ends of the ribs meet and centered between top and back. It should be reamed to about five-sixteenths inch. The endpin is then matched to the taper of the hole. It must fit tightly because it is not glued in.

Step Fourteen — The Fingerboard and Nut

Either buy or make a fingerboard. If made, refer to the woods list for size of wood block needed and type of wood. Take a different piece of wood the length of the neck and shaped to cradle the rounded neck. This will be used as a clampin' tool.

Use a fingerboard pattern, the width of the neck at the nut and widened with a straight taper to one-and-a-half inches at the other end, and trace it onto the wood block.

Saw out the fingerboard and sand the side to be glued to the neck perfectly flat and smooth.

The fingerboard surface is rounded, side-to-side, from the nut to the bottom end and sanded smooth.

Photo: Sterling Flagg

Next, the underside part of the fingerboard that extends out over the top is hollowed out. Glue the finger-board to the neck with wood glue. Be sure that it stays in place because it is a flat surface and will move easily until hard-ened. After cor-rect placement is assured, cradle the neck assembly in the wood block made to use as a clampin' tool. Put a piece of leather on the top of the fingerboard and clamp it in place usin' two clamps and allow it to dry for three hours.

Nut

Fingerboard and nut

The nut is a one-fourth-inch square block of hard maple, persimmon, or dogwood, the width of the fin-gerboard at the scroll end. After trimmin' to size, glue in the nut, then shape to match arch of the fingerboard leavin' it about one-sixteenth inch above the finger-board.

Once the strings are added, notches will be cut in the nut for each string.

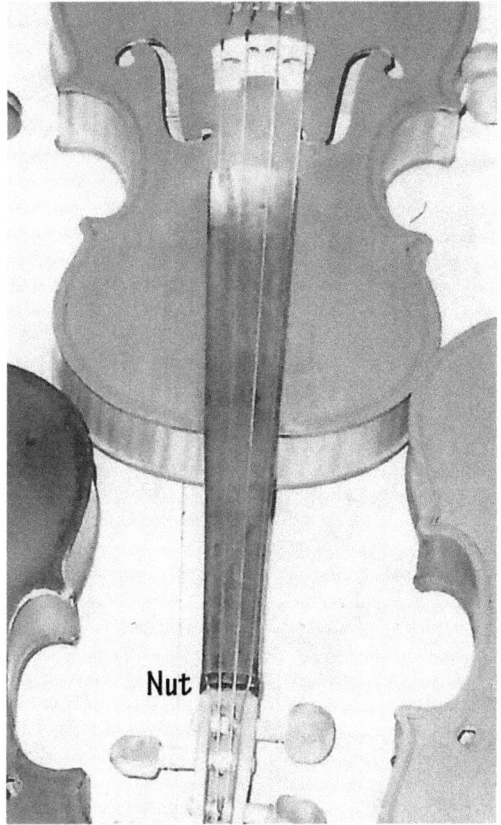

Fingerboard

Tailpiece

End pin

Step Fifteen — Finishing

All removable pieces should be set aside for sandin' the fiddle. Always sand with the grain of the wood — never across it. Start with coarse sandpaper and sand all surfaces, graduatin' to finer sandpaper each time all surfaces are sanded and eventually endin' with 600-grade paper. Then use a piece of flannel to polish the wood, rubbin' with the grain all over the instrument.

Once smooth, finish with up to four coats of Tru-oil, rubbed on lightly with a cloth or a used dryer sheet and allow each coat to dry. The instrument could be rubbed again with a clean, dry flannel cloth between coats. Always rub with the grain. Stain or varnish to the builder's taste.

Step Sixteen — The Tailpiece

The tailpiece can be bought or made. Refer to beginnin' chart for wood type and block size. Also needed are a tail line and four fine tuners. The tailpiece will be rounded the same as the fingerboard on top and it will be hollowed out on the underside of the big end. Then drill four holes in the big end for the tuners with a one-eighth-inch drill bit. Holes will be drilled in the small end for the tail line with a bit just bigger than a one-sixteenth-inch bit.

On the back side of the two holes, on the underneath side of the tailpiece, there has to be a notch for the end of tail line to rest in. Attach tail line and assemble fine tuners into the tailpiece. Once cut to shape, it will be fastened to the end pin with a copper wire or gut tail line.

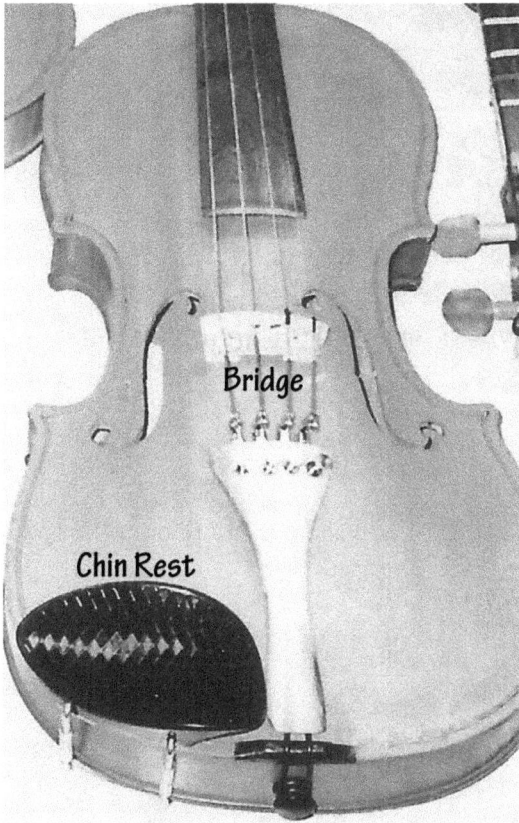

Step Seventeen — The Bridge

Buy a bridge. The bridge usually comes too tall. Shape it to match the arch of the fingerboard and tailpiece so that the strings are about a one-eighth inch from the fingerboard.

The bridge will be put in place after the strings are attached and tightened.

Step Eighteen —The Chin Rest

These can be purchased. They are placed on the left side of tailpiece on the top.

Step Nineteen — Reassembly

Attach the tailpiece with the tail line; place a potholder underneath so the fine tuners will not scratch the top.

Attach the violin G string (fourth) to the left side of the tailpiece and run up to the first peg nearest the nut on the left side of the neck. Wrap counterclockwise around peg inside the tunin' box and then repeat with E string (first) in the right side of the tailpiece and attached to the first right peg, wrappin' clockwise, then the D string (third) left and finally the A string (second) right.

Place the bridge underneath the strings and tighten the strings just enough to hold the bridge in place while positionin' it in the center of the F holes.

With a ruler measure about one-sixteenth-inch from the outside of the nut on each side and use a small wedge-shaped file to cut grooves for the E and G strings to cross over. Then cut equally spaced notches for the A and D strings between those two strings.

On the bridge, the E and G grooves will be cut about one-eighth inch from the outside with the A and D string grooves equally spaced in between.

Step Twenty — The Sound Post

With the strings just tight enough to hold the bridge in place, set the sound post.

The sound post is a pine rod one-fourth inch in diameter, and just long enough to be wedged in between front and back. It is placed under the first and second strings towards the big end of the fiddle just behind the bridge. It takes a little trial and error to get it in the right spot.

Then slowly tighten all four strings equally, eventually bringin' them up to standard 440 pitch.

Step Twenty-One — Enjoy!

The fiddle is ready to play or learn to play. Find a safe place to keep it after all that work!

Some of Violet Hensley's fiddles

Discography

"I never thought I was good enough to record anything." Violet Hensley

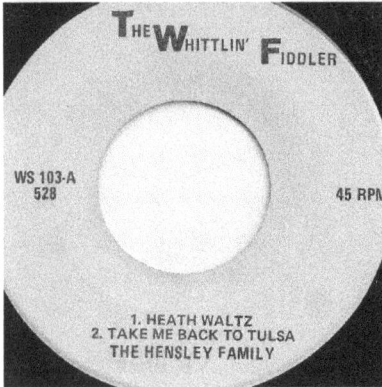

The Whittling Fiddler — The Hensley Family
45 RPM — WS103 A and B (528) EP
Recorded: 1969
Where: Wayne Raney's Studio in Dardanelle, Arkansas

Musicians:
Violet Hensley — fiddle
Adren Hensley — guitar
Sandra Hensley — guitar
Lewonna Hensley — jawbone

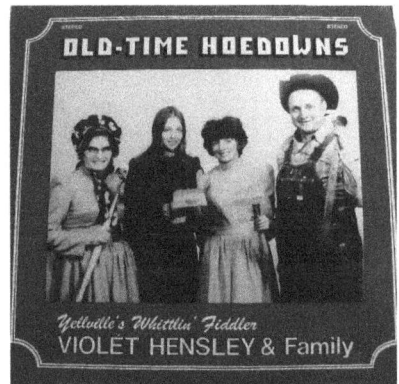

Side A
Soldier's Joy
Cindy
Side B
Heath Waltz
Take Me Back To Tulsa

Old Time Hoedowns — Yellville's Whitting Fiddler — Violet Hensley and Family
LP — 999967
Recorded: 1973
Where: John's Recording — Russellville, Arkansas

Musicians:
Violet Hensley – fiddle
Adren Hensley – guitar
Sandra Hensley – guitar
Lewonna Hensley – jawbone

Side One
Turkey in the Straw
Nellie Gray

Paddy, Won't You Drink Some Cider
She'll Be Coming 'Round the Mountain
Buffalo Girls
Soldier's Joy
Side Two
D Waltz (Waltz of the Violets)
Liberty
Green Valley Waltz
San Antonio Rose
Eighth of January
Boil Them Cabbage Down

Old Time Fiddle Tunes Violet Hensley by Yellville's Whittling Fiddler
LP — Red White and Bluegrass Records
BG — 05 Stereo 33 1/3 rpm; CD — 2003
No number
Recorded: 1979
Where: Cedar Crest Studios, Mountain Home, Arkansas
Engineer: Bob Ketchum

Musicians:
Violet Hensley — fiddle
Adren Hensley — flat top guitar
Sandra (Hensley) Flagg — flat top guitar and fiddle sticks
Lewonna (Hensley) Nelson — plays jawbone (jackassaphone) and flat top guitar
Tim Nelson — five-string banjo and bass guitar

Side One
Lost Indian
Old Joe Clark
Turkey in the Straw
Train Whistle Blues
Boil Them Cabbage Down
One Eyed Gopher

Side Two

Take Me Back to Tulsa
Arkansas Traveler
Golden Slippers
Jericho
Walk Along John
Healthy (Heath) Waltz

Whittling Fiddler and Family — Music by Violet Hensley

Cassette, CD — 2003 No number
Recorded: 1986
Where: Caravel Studios, Branson, Missouri

Music by Violet Hensley
"The Whittling Fiddler"
and Family

Musicians:

Violet Hensley — fiddle
Adren Hensley — flat top guitar
Sandra (Hensley) Flagg — acoustic guitar and fiddle sticks
Lewonna (Hensley) Nelson — plays jawbone
Tim Nelson — bass guitar

Buffalo Nickel
Sally Gooden
Ragtime Annie
One Eyed Gopher
Faded Love
Going Up Brushy Fork
Down Yonder
Cindy
Sally Ann
Peek-A-Boo Waltz
Walk Along John
She'll Be Coming 'Round the Mountain
Jericho
Boil Them Cabbage Down
Wildwood Flower

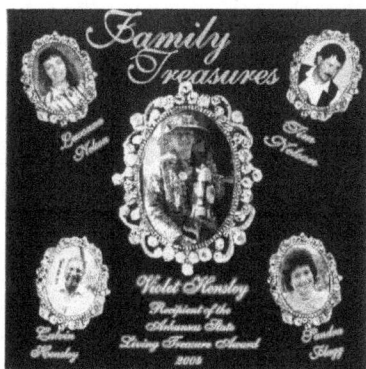

Family Treasures — Violet Hensley
Recipient of Arkansas State Living
Treasure Award 2004
CD — No number
Recorded: April 4, 2004
Where: Stone County Recording Studio,
Crane, Missouri
Engineer: Greg Bailey

Musicians:
Violet Hensley — fiddle, vocals
Calvin Hensley — guitar
Sandra (Hensley) Flagg — guitar and fiddle sticks
Lewonna (Hensley) Nelson — percussion (plays jawbone and guitar)
Tim Nelson – bass guitar

Note: First album including Violet's singing

Soldier's Joy
Red Wing
Sugar in the Coffee (Sugar in My Coffee-O)
Marmaduke's Hornpipe
Sweet Fern
8th of January
Black Eyed Susie
Bonaparts (Bonaparte's) Retreat
Chicken Reel
Angeline the Baker
Nellie Gray
Little Brown Jug
Put Your Little Foot
Wagoner
Shortening (Shortenin') Bread
D Waltz
Liberty
Hold Fast to the Right

Wang Wang Blues Violet Hensley
CD No number
Recorded: July 31, 2007 and August 1, 2007
Where: Panther Creek Recording, Yellville, Arkansas
Engineer: Steve Kuether

Musicians:
Violet Hensley — fiddle, vocals
Calvin Hensley — acoustic guitar
Sandra (Hensley) Flagg — acoustic guitar and fiddle sticks
Lewonna (Hensley) Nelson — horse's jawbone
Tim Nelson — electric bass

Cripple Creek
Paddy, Won't You Drink Some Cider?
Green Valley Waltz
Black Eyed Suzie
Good Bye My Lover, Good Bye (Tuning: DADD)
Wang Wang Blues
Battle of New Orleans
Fill My Way with Love
Old Dan Tucker
Rabbit, Where's Your Mama?
Rose Nell
Pop Goes the Weasel
Waltz of the Violets
Deep Elm Blues
Haste to the Wedding
Skip to My Lou

To order Violet Hensley music, visit www.VioletHensley.com, or write Violet Hensley, P.O. Box 484, Yellville, AR 72687.

Traditional Fiddle Music of the Ozarks Vol. 1 — North American Tradition Series
CD Rounder CD 0435
Also features fiddlers Stan Jackson, Gene Goforth, Howe Teague, Bob Holt, Jesse Wallace, Cecil Goforth, Sam Younger and Audrey Handle.
Recorded: 1997
Where: Violet Hensley house
Producers: Gordon McCann and Mark Wilson

Musicians:
Violet Hensley — fiddle, vocals
Sandra (Hensley) Flagg — acoustic guitar and fiddle sticks
Lewonna (Hensley) Nelson — horse's jawbone

Jericho
Uncle Henry
Rose Nell
Sam Moore Waltz
Wang Wang Blues
Mate to the Hog Waltz

Violet Hensley and producer Gordon McCann play a tune in 1997.

Violet Hensley and her musical family in 1979. From left are (front) Lewonna (Hensley) Nelson, Violet, (back) Tim Nelson, Adren Hensley, and Sandra (Hensley) Flagg.

Glen Campbell and Violet fiddle around with one of her fiddles backstage in 1996.

Sources – fiddle tunes

Violet Hensley has taught ten students fiddle, including three from her family.

George Washington Brumley (1928–1933)

"Arkansas Traveler"
"Black Eyed Suzy" — *I learned the words at different times, different places.*
"Buffalo Girls" — *A lot of folks call it "Buffalo Gals."*
"Buffalo Nickel" — *He also called it "Chinquapin" also "Chinkapin." I've heard other fiddlers call it "Bug-Eyed Rabbit," "Lead Out," and "Crooked Stove Pipe."*
"Cindy"
"Cripple Creek" — *I learned it better though as time went on.*
"Eighth of January"
"Haste to the Wedding"
"Goodbye My Lover, Goodbye" — *(Played with a tuning: DADD) I remember him singin' the words, "Goodbye My Lover, Goodbye." I later heard it called "Uncle Henry."*
"Green Valley Waltz"
"Jericho"
"Little Brown Jug" — *I got the words from other people. He knew some words. That is the tune I forgot to put the verse in about the cow when I recorded it.*
"Mate to the Hog Waltz" — *My dad played one called the "Hog Waltz" and then he played another one, which had notes similar, he called it the "Mate to the Hog Waltz." I once heard Junior Chambers play the "Hog Waltz" but he called it "Barbed Wire."*
"Old Joe Clark"
"Soldier's Joy" — *This recording will be closer to the way my dad played than I do the tunes today because I have added other bow work and notes over the years.*
"Turkey in the Straw" — *I learned it in key of G and played it for the square dances.*
"Paddy Won't You Drink Some Cider" — *He would sing, "You be the hoss and I'll be the rider. We go to Buddy Martin's and get some cider. Paddy won't you drink some, Paddy won't you drink some, Paddy won't you drink some, good ole cider."*
"Pop Goes the Weasel" — *My dad played that; I just improved it.*
"Rose Nell" — *That was the very first tune I learned to play on the fiddle.*
"Sally Gooden" — *I learned that from my dad and also Uncle Jim Pettitt*

in the early 1930s. Dad would always include these words between fiddle rounds: "If I had a piece of pie or I had a piece of pudding, I'd give them all away to see Sally Gooden."

"Shortening Bread" — *I learned to play it different later in life.*

"Skip to My Lou" — *We used to play this tune for square dances, but they called it a party tune. Some families wouldn't let girls go to dances but they could go to play parties.*

"Sugar in the Coffee" — *He would add the words: "How in the world does the old folks know that I love sugar in my coffee-o?"*

"Wagoner" — *He used to call it "Tennessee Wagoner."*

"Walk Along John" — *When dad would perform "Walk Along John," he would sing these words: "Walk Along John with your paper collar on. If you ever get it off, you will never get it on." That is only words I ever remember him sayin' to that.*

Uncle Jim Pettitt (1930–1932)

"After the Ball"

"Black Eyed Susie" — *I got the words for "Black Eyed Susie" later from a book or hearin' it on a record.*

"Chicken Reel" — *I had to relearn it after puttin' the fiddle up. He put a real high note in it. I couldn't find it until I learned it again from Dusty and Speck Rhodes sister — Bea Hitt.*

"D Waltz (Waltz of the Violets)" — *I learned some words to it later.*

"Deep Elm Blues"

"Down Yonder" — *I played it some when I was younger.*

"Durang's Hornpipe"

"Fire on the Mountain"

"Green Valley Waltz"

"Heath Waltz" — *I think I play it today just the same as I learned it back then.*

"Nellie Gray"

"Old Dan Tucker" — *Uncle Jim and my dad*

"Red Wing"

"Sally Ann" — *Dad played it too, but Uncle Jim could play it better. Dad played with a stiffer arm.*

"Sweet Bunch of Daisies"

"Tom and Jerry"

"Train Whistle Blues"

244 / Whittlin' and Fiddlin' My Own Way

"Wang Wang Blues"

<u>**Sam Moore (1930–35)**</u>

"Sam Moore Waltz"

<u>**Uncle Jack Brumley**</u>

"Uncle Jack's Tune"

<u>**Community:**</u>

"Battle of New Orleans" — *on that tune, I started it as "Eighth of January" and ended it with the battle of New Orleans. I learned the bowin' for the "Battle of New Orleans" from listenin' to Jimmy Driftwood sing it.*
"Boil Them Cabbage Down" — *I picked this one up at music gatherin's in the 1950s or 60s hearin' different folks playin' and singin' it.*
"Hold Fast to the Right" — *I been playin' that one for quite a while. Don't remember where I got it.*
"Lost Indian" — *I learned that off another fiddler at a gatherin'.*
"Marmaduke's Hornpipe" — *I learned that one from a record by fiddler Lonnie Roberts. I learned that in one afternoon.*
"One-Eyed Gopher" — *I learned that one in 1973. Mr. Krutcher of Farmerville, Louisiana, saw "On the Road with Charles Kuralt," and came by to visit. I had an old five-string banjo that I loaned him and he took back home. He had us come down to his house, and he put us up and paid for the room, gas, and meals. An older fiddler, which I can't remember his name, came to the jam session that he hosted and played this tune. I recorded it on my little recorder and brought it back and learned it.*
"Peek-A-Boo Waltz" — *Fiddler Cliff Trizzler was good at that one. He also played at Silver Dollar City and I learned it from listenin' and recordin' it from him playin' it. He was four years older than me.*
"Put Your Little Foot" — *It came from listenin' to other people play.*
"Ragtime Annie" — *I learned it at Silver Dollar City in 1981. I had the tune in my head, and I used to whistle the tunes. I couldn't get the high parts just right on that one, but I made it match with the guitar players.*
"San Antonio Rose" — *I didn't do a good job on that one. It was incomplete. I learned it from playin' at gatherin's with friends at different homes*

in the 1950s. This was a song often sang by Ray and Obeda Fisk, and although Obeda sang it correctly, only the portion I recorded stuck with me. I didn't remember how they played the complete tune until much later.

"She'll Be Coming 'Round the Mountain" — *It came along from hearin' people sing it. I don't remember when I put it on the fiddle. We heard it sung when I was a teenager. I put it on the fiddle from them singin' it.*

"Sweet Fern" — *I learned that from Tillman Pyatt. He came down for me to fix his fiddle. I played it, and he said, "You learned that off my tape. and you do a better job than I do."*

Radio, recordings or hymnal:

"Angeline the Baker" — *This song played through the speaker system on a tape in the morning before the openin' at Silver Dollar City in the 1990s. The tune ran over and over, and I got it in my head from hearing it so much.*

"Bonaparte's Retreat" — *I learned that one off a record, probably Pee Wee King.*

"Faded Love" — *Verl Doshier wanted me to learn it and loaned me a record by Bob Wills.*

"Fill My Way With Love" — *From the church hymnal in 1943 Vesta Heights Hill, also called Tin Can Hill, Hot Springs, Arkansas.*

"Going Up Brushy Fork" — *I learned that from a Kessinger Brothers record.*

"Golden Slippers" — *I heard it from a feller that played at Silver Dollar City. I later found it on record and learned to play it.*

"Liberty" — *I learned that since I started work at Silver Dollar City. I got it from hearin' people playing and listening to records.*

"Take Me Back From Tulsa" — *I learned it from hearing it on the radio in the 1960s. I heard Bob Wills and the Texas Playboys play it but I did not try to play it just like they did.*

"Wildwood Flower" — *That is one that I heard originally on a Carter Family record. I play it a little differently than they did.*

Violet Hensley shows her number five (1961) (left)
and number four (1934) fiddles in 1961.

About the co-author

Randall Franks

© 2011 Randall Franks Media – Teryl Jackson

Actor/entertainer Randall Franks is best known as "Officer Randy Goode" from TV's "In the Heat of the Night," a role he performed on NBC and CBS from 1988–1993. He also starred with Robert Townsend in the series "Musical Theater of Hope" airing on GMC (Gospel Music Channel).

He has co-starred or starred in fifteen films with superstars including Dolly Parton, Christian Slater, William Hurt, and Stella Parton, and legendary western star "Doc" Tommy Scott. His most recent film is "Lukewarm" with John Schneider, Nicole Gale Anderson, and Bill Cobbs.

Franks' musical stylings have been heard in 150 countries and by more than twenty-five million Americans. The Independent Country Music Hall of Fame member's musical career boasts nineteen album releases, nineteen singles, and over two hundred recordings with artists from various genres. The International Bluegrass Music Museum Legend annually hosts the historic Grand Master Fiddler Championship at the Country Music Hall of Fame in Nashville, Tenn. The award-winning fiddler's best-selling release, "Handshakes and Smiles," was a top twenty Christian music seller. Many of his albums were among the top 30 bluegrass recordings of their release year. The Atlanta Country Music Hall of Fame member shared a top country vocal collaboration with Grand Ole Opry stars the Whites. In addition to his solo career, which includes thirteen years guest starring for the Grand Ole Opry, Franks is a former member of Bill Monroe's Blue Grass Boys and Jim and Jesse's Virginia Boys. He has performed with Jeff and Sheri Easter, the Lewis Family, the Marksmen Quartet, the Watkins Family, Elaine and Shorty Eager, "Doc" Tommy Scott's Last Real Old Time Medicine Show, and Doodle and the Golden River Grass.

He serves on the Ringgold City Council in Ringgold, Georgia, and is past chairman of the Catoosa Citizens for Literacy, which assists individuals in learning to read and pursuing a GED at its Catoosa County Learning Center near Ringgold. He is also president of the Share America

Foundation, Inc. that provides the Pearl and Floyd Franks Scholarship to musicians continuing the traditional music of Appalachia. He hosts a monthly concert series at the historic Ringgold Depot to fund the scholarships. He is the Northwest Georgia Joint Economic Development Authority film industry liaison. He also serves as Georgia Production Partnership secretary.

He authored five other books including, "Encouragers I — Finding the Light;" "A Mountain Pearl: Appalachian Reminiscing and Recipes;" "Stirring Up Success with a Southern Flavor," and "Stirring Up Additional Success with a Southern Flavor" with Shirley Smith; and "Snake Oil, Superstars and Me" with "Doc" Tommy Scott and Shirley Swiesz. A journalist with more than twenty state and national awards, Franks is also a syndicated columnist with his "Southern Style" appearing weekly in newspapers from North Carolina to Texas and at http://randall-franks.com/. He was included among his generation's leading country humorists in the Loyal Jones book "Country Music Humorists and Comedians."

For more information, visit www.randallfranks.com and www.shareamericafoundation.org.

Randall Franks and Violet Hensley at Silver Dollar City in 2011

Index

Violet Hensley in 1979

www.ingramcontent.com/pod-product-compliance
Lightning Source LLC
Chambersburg PA
CBHW060303100426
42742CB00011B/1854